SAYING HELLO TO YOUR LIFE AFTER GRIEF

Smyth & Helwys Publishing, Inc.
6316 Peake Road
Macon, Georgia 31210-3960
1-800-747-3016
©2004 by Smyth & Helwys Publishing
All rights reserved.
Printed in the United States of America.

The paper used in this publication meets the minimum requirements of
American National Standard for Information Sciences—
Permanence of Paper for Printed Library Materials.
ANSI Z39.48–1984. (alk. paper)

Library of Congress Cataloging-in-Publication Data

Clemons, Hardy.
Saying hello to your life after grief /
by Hardy Clemons
p. cm.
Includes bibliographical references.
ISBN 1-57312-439-7 (pbk. : alk. paper)
1. Grief—Religious aspects of Christianity.
I. Title.
BV4905.3.C54 2004
248.8'66—dc22

2004007182

Hardy Clemons

Foreword by Wayne Oates

Saying Hello
to Your *Life*
After Grief

SMYTH&HELWYS
PUBLISHING, INCORPORATED · MACON, GEORGIA

Dedication

To Ardelle—friend, wife, and partner
in ministry—and to Kay Clemons Watt—our
daughter in whom we are well pleased and my
colleague in the ministry of
pastoral counseling.

Contents

Foreword

Veteran pastor Hardy Clemons has culled his experiences with grief into this easy-to-read volume. Like birth and death, grief is an inescapable but inherent part of life. This book is not a cumbersome textbook or a sentimental, soothing book. Instead, it is a book packed with stories, poems, Scriptures, and specific guidance for a grieving person. Its simple words speak to every person's grieving heart and burdened life. Clemons addresses loss through death, divorce, growing up, job changes, and other struggles people face.

Those who minister to the grieving will find resources of comfort to offer. Ministers grieve too, and this book can help them work through the grief they feel over a conflicted congregation, dismissal from their position, or other troubles that affect the church. Hardy Clemons has written both for laypeople and for ministers.

This is not merely a foreword to Hardy Clemons's book. I have suffered through grief alongside him. He speaks of the death of Grady Nutt, our mutual friend who died in a plane crash. He and I shared in that loss and comforted each other. We also shared in the loss of Laura Lue, John Claypool's daughter. Hardy Clemons and I have been friends and confidantes for four decades. He has comforted me through life's losses, such as my mother's death and my changing job.

Clemons writes specific stories that clarify each of his points. They are fresh, real, and moving stories. *Saying Hello to Your Life After Grief* [formerly *Saying Goodbye to Your Grief*] is an adventure in narrative theology. This is especially true of the interpretation of Samuel's grief over Saul described in 1 Samuel 16 (vv. 48ff). I recommend this book to the broken-hearted and to those who would comfort them. Family members can read it and find ways to connect during times when communication suffers due to sadness. As Tennyson wrote, grief has "no language but a cry

Wayne E. Oates
Louisville, Kentucky

Introduction

Writing a book that offers help for a grieving person is courageous at best and arrogant at worst. God knows we have already enough arrogance. What we need is an humble, intentional willingness to listen—to God and each other—and to communicate about our common grief.

To walk into another person's loss and grief is to stand on sacred ground. It is sensitive and respectful to "take off our shoes" in such surroundings. To presume that we know what the grieving person is experiencing or that we can tell them how to fix their grief—or another's grief—approaches ministerial malpractice.

No one can write a book without amassing an incalculable debt to family members, colleagues, church people, and friends. I am no exception. This book is the result of more than forty years of pastoral and personal pilgrimage. In the early 1970s, I contracted with Dr. Wayne Oates in the Psychology of Religion department at the Southern Baptist Theological Seminary and with the School of Psychiatry at the University of Louisville Medical School to spend a month on sabbatical leave from Second Baptist Church in Lubbock, Texas. Among other things, Dr. Oates agreed to help me address the daunting subject of grief.

In that regard, I owe an everlasting debt to Dr. Oates and his colleagues—Clarence Barton, Dr. John Boyle, Dr. Swan Haworth, and Dr. Elizabeth Hutchens—for their patient, probing tutelage and friendship. They took this almost burned out "thirty-something" pastor and helped me find my way into a healthier model for dealing with spiritual struggles—whether mine or someone else's. Wayne and I first met in 1956 in Alpine, Texas, where he led a retreat for Baptist campus ministers. I responded to his gracious wisdom as a dry, weary traveler to an oasis.

I had never been exposed to the combination of insightful grace, professional competence, and biblical acumen Wayne offered. My heart sang as he taught us that sharing God's good news with people meant more than giving them spiritual laws, telling them "The Story," or involving them in the best new creative programming designed to build a larger crowd. He taught me to listen, ask honest questions, treat people as the valuable children of God they are, listen more, and then faithfully walk with them as fellow travelers on a journey toward wholeness.

From that weekend to his death on October 21, 1999, Wayne was my teacher, mentor, fellow pastor, and faithful friend. To my great delight and profit, we communicated by mail, telephone, and in person throughout those years. That he entered my life three months into my ministry and exited it three months before my retirement is an interesting irony. Moreover, the fact that he began his journey in Poe Mill Village in Greenville, South Carolina, the city where I have served for the past fifteen years, provides a sturdy set of bookends for the living library that has nurtured, informed, and facilitated my journey. I miss Wayne mightily!

Another set of colleagues has also made foundational contributions to the development of this book. First, the venturesome Baptist-Christians at "Second B" in Lubbock were my pastors for twenty-one years as much as I was theirs. Just into my thirties, I joined their vision to continue building a different kind of West Texas church in the late 1960s. They wanted us to build together a church that genuinely practiced what they called a "corporate ministry." As described by the Apostle Paul in 1 Corinthians 12, this "ministry of the body to the body with Christ as the head" had no room for pedestals of privilege or prominence. We learned that ministry, in life or loss, is not about status. It is about "function"—doing what we are created and called by God to do—wherein we serve as "laborers together under God."

Through our multiple struggles with life and faith, this people of God lived out the concept of partnership ministry and taught me that it is acceptable for a pastor to grieve his own losses as well as offer care to them as they grieve. Part of this involved respecting differences and diversities among us. We encouraged each other to grieve in our own unique ways. Another part was to be honest with each other in sharing our common humanity. Our fellowship was an open, authentic community of faith rather than an exercise in ecclesiastical game-playing. I returned from my time in Louisville to find a diaconate, staff, and congregation who were eager to understand and employ whatever wisdom we could garner for helping each other with our mutual growth challenges and grief.

Furthermore, the pastoral staff at Second B became a colloquium of partners in ministry who labored to articulate and impart the wisdom and courage associated with grief work. We sought to help each other—as various body parts cooperate together—in our general spiritual development as well as our specific journeys into and beyond the various forms of grief. The original pastoral staff that addressed this issue included Larry Douglas, Curtis Driver, Beth Pennington, Dot Thompson, Robert Wells, and myself. We did indeed "labor together under God," seeking to apply these insights to the people we served. Later, other colleagues joined us—Philip Christopher, John Claypool, Michelle McClendon, Gary West, Dan Williams, and others. As partnering pastors, they honed each other's attempts to "be there" for members of the congregation and community, as well as for each other in facing the shock, agony, and loneliness of grief. I owe these colleagues and friends an immense debt of gratitude.

Additionally, the venerable congregation known as First Baptist Greenville, South Carolina—an authentic team of partners in ministry itself—has shared this sacred quest. As with all congregations, they wrestled in the years before we joined them with a litany of disappointment and loss. They received Ardelle and me as though we were long-lost relatives when we arrived in 1988. Together we forged our way into owning our grief and sharing our feelings with each other, so that we might say goodbye to grief and come forth into the light of a new day. This historic church—which was a Baptist church before the Southern Baptist Convention existed—shared in a valiant and gracious way its struggles with denominational loss and the massive personal and church family losses that come to us all.

The pastoral team in Greenville added their unique insights to what was formulated in Lubbock. Over a period of nearly a dozen years, Glen Adkins, Don Flowers, Donna Forrester, Janice Johnson, Michelle McClendon, Don Rose, Frank Smith, Bill Thomas, Mary Wrye, and Baxter Wynn were faithful colleagues as this material came together in its present form. The Greenville congregation and these veteran fellow pastors have ministered to me as much as I to them, for which I am profoundly grateful.

To fail to mention Dr. Charles Mahone would be a grievous oversight. Senior Professor of Psychology at Texas Tech University and a practicing clinical psychologist, he teamed with Dr. Oates in supervising my fledgling efforts to gain competence as a pastoral counselor. He walked with me as fellow pilgrim, fellow churchman, and friend as I sharpened my skills and earned credentials as a pastoral counselor and supervisor.

Also, Marlea Rhem, psychologist at Greenville Psychiatric Associates, first came to me for supervision in her desire to become credentialed as a pastoral counselor. She quickly became my trusted colleague and friend. She pored over this material and made innumerable creative suggestions as we sought to comfort the grieving and address our own grief. To travel this journey with her, to witness how she faced her own enormous losses, to bask in the valiant zest she had for being alive and the gallant way she faced her death in summer 2003 was a sacred education for me.

Finally, my wife and partner in ministry, Ardelle, and our beloved daughter, Kay Clemons Watt, have walked these trails in sensitive, insightful, and supportive ways. They have joined with my parents, H. P. and Kathleen Clemons, and Ardelle's parents, E. F. and Vera Hallock, in forming a cauldron of care for the intellectual, emotional, and action-oriented initiatives of finding grace and new opportunities amid the rubble of disappointment and loss.

This book is not a textbook about grief. It is more personal than that. It is written to people in grief more than to anyone else. I must add that it can be read too soon in one's process of growing through grief. At first in dealing with grief, we are often not ready to embrace or even hear much about God's promise of new life. Loss is too consuming for that! I see the book as an invitation to begin identifying your losses, assessing their gravity, owning your feelings about them, embracing (rather than avoiding or denying) the associated pain, and then, in the grace and strength of God, to become what Henri Nowen taught us to call a "wounded healer" as we journey toward the sunset of our earthly sojourns.

May I wish you God speed and good journey as you look toward whatever grief brought you to this book. May I assure you that my prayers are with you as you seek to respond to God's gift of new life. I pray that in the fullness of time, you will walk through your own "valley of the shadow" as Jesus walked through his temptation experiences, the betrayal and relinquishment of Gethsemane, the agony and loneliness of Calvary, and into his own God-given victory of new life in resurrection.

Hardy Clemons
Greenville, South Carolina
November 2003

Chapter One

The Anatomy of Grief

Grief has brought agony to human beings since Adam and Eve lost the Garden of Eden. One of the most excruciating experiences of life, grief existed at the beginning. Yet, we waited until the middle of the twentieth century before writing intentionally about the subject.

Since the mid-1940s, more specific help has been available, but we still have much to learn about working through grief. May we be willing to learn, trust, grow, and work.

We dare not be glib in the face of grief—neither our own nor that of others. Grief is individual; no one person's grief is exactly like another's.

Grief is awful, particularly when it is your own. Lord Byron was right: he saw the reality of grief as "the solitude of pain—the feeling that your heart is in pieces; your mind is a blank; there's not a joy the world can give like that it takes away."[1]

Any loss causes grief. Any loss! The more closely a person is bonded with the person or object of loss, the more bereft the person feels from that loss. Regardless of how others perceive a loss, it is devastating to the one who experiences it. Someone who does not understand your loss can easily make flippant comments: "Get over it!" "My grief was worse than that!" "We'll get you another dog." However, we must take seriously the fact that significant loss always causes significant pain.

During my first pastorate, my secretary called and said, "Shirley's second cousin has just died; she is devastated. She needs her pastor!" I rushed to Shirley's home willingly, but I did not understand why a second cousin was such a serious loss. On the way I tried to think of how a second cousin is related to a person. Did I know any of my second cousins?

When I arrived, I quickly learned that Shirley's parents had died in an auto accident when she was five years old. The "second cousin" was the woman who took her in, offered her a home, and mothered her all those years. Shirley had remained close to this woman while growing into adulthood. The family records and the obituary listed "second cousin," but Shirley's heart cried "Mommy!" Of course, I know now that the loss of Shirley's second mother brought back to her conscious mind the loss of her first mommy. Superficially, her loss sounded insignificant to a young pastor. Actually, she grieved a major loss *and* a double loss! We must be hesitant to assume we know what someone is feeling as the result of a loss we consider insignificant. We need to understand as much as possible about the anatomy of grief.

Eric Lindeman gave us a wonderful gift when he began his research following the tragic Coconut Grove fire in Boston in 1944. He approached the families who had lost loved ones in the fire one by one and—with care, skill, and patient sensitivity—listened to their experiences. He kept careful notes and then recorded his findings to help others struggling with loss and the people seeking to be there for them. He documented what Wayne Oates phrased so well years later: "To go through grief, we must grow through grief."[2]

The world has struggled with loss since Eden and the death of Abel, but not until 1944 did anyone document what tends to happen to humans when we experience loss. Not until 1970 did an American medical school include a textbook on grief in its curriculum.

This latency may have been born of denial. We do not want to face our losses. My friend "Red" Duke—surgeon at the University of Texas Health Sciences Center in Houston, instigator of helicopter ambulances, and star of his own medical-help TV spot—said it well: "Denial is not a river in Egypt." Maybe we humans are so good at avoiding pain and the labor of grief that we did not want to face the causes and remedies. Maybe we trusted in folk cures too long. At any rate, we waited unnecessarily to have the knowledge now available about moving through grief.

The crux of the knowledge is that any and all loss causes grief—the more serious the loss, the more painful the grief. I invite you to consider some of the many losses that comprise the anatomy of grief. I hope you will find help and encouragement for working through your story of grief and for listening as others work through their stories. The great Miguel de Unamuno helped us learn that we begin to heal from grief when we walk out into the streets and become willing to "share our common griefs."

Death of Someone Close to You

Death is not the only cause of grief, but it is probably the most prevalent and the first to come to mind. Of course, there are varying degrees of loss and varying degrees of grief surrounding loss through death.

Sudden, unexpected death is more difficult to grieve. When death slips into a nursing home in the still of night after a long, debilitating illness, grief is still present. I learned when my mother died in 1983 after a long illness that death can be a terrific shock even when it is not a surprise. However, sudden, surprising death causes a shock more toxic to our well-being than expected death. Numbness usually continues longer with sudden death than with a death we anticipate.

Grief we experience from the death of someone bonded to us is more severe than when that person is an acquaintance or even a friend. Grief can surprise caregivers because, as we have seen, relationships are not always what they seem.

How someone dies also affects how we grieve. When we cannot or choose not to see the body of the deceased, coming to grips with the reality of death can be more difficult and more prolonged. People unnecessarily fear remembering the person as he or she appears in the casket. Regardless of whether we view the body, after the shock of death abates, our memories usually cluster around active life and pleasant situations more than around images of death. Violent death tends to occasion a more severe grief. If the body is mangled beyond recognition, or in cases of murder or suicide, grief seems harder to grow through.

Grief resulting from the death of someone from whom we were estranged at the time or with whom we had positive or negative unfinished business can be harder to sustain.

Please do not forget about animals. Some people have animals who are family members. Their deaths feel like the deaths of dear friends and are sometimes more difficult to grieve—particularly since many people fail to understand why grieving owners feel no comfort by the suggestion that "we'll get you another dog."

Furthermore, we need to stay alert to the possibility that a "lesser grief" may occasion an emotional deluge that is actually tied to an earlier, "greater," but still unresolved grief.

Divorce

Some people who have experienced both death and divorce report that divorce can be a harder grief to bear. Death has a final reality that divorce does not. Most divorces do not simply occur. The majority of couples try repeatedly to save the marriage. They separate and then reconcile, sometimes repeatedly, which elongates the loss and grief. All the while, grief multiplies for everyone concerned. I heard the great Carl Whitaker, one of the gurus of family systems therapy, say categorically, "There is no such thing as divorce."[3]

Divorce creates loss for everyone! The person who does not want the divorce may feel rejection. The person who wants it may feel failure. Children lose their parents. Grandparents lose their beloved in-laws. Friends have difficulty being friends with each member of the couple afterward. Everyone loses, but society does not respond as with death. Grief may go unnoticed and hence hide underground. Few people, even in a caring environment, bring casseroles, send cards, or make a call when divorce occurs.

In my experience, one of the most severe griefs I have known was that of a grandmother when her beloved grandson was divorced from her granddaughter-in-law, the apple of her eye. She loved her dearly. They had truly bonded! After a messy divorce, the grandmother was by default estranged from the "daughter she had always wanted but never had." She groaned in agony and soon died. Grief can be terminal.

I know many adults who have never resolved the pain and grief that occurred when their parents divorced. People have said to me for years, "We're going to wait until the children go to college before we divorce. We don't want to upset them." My experience is that adult children have as much difficulty with divorce as younger children—sometimes more! To watch your home split right after you launch from it into a new and insecure world can be ultimately traumatic.

Loss of a Job

My fifty-seven-year-old friend/deacon called me right after work one day. "I've been fired," he announced. He had worked with the same company more than twenty years, but a larger group had recently acquired it. He was fifteen days short of having his retirement vested. "They called me in at 3:30 and told me to clean out my desk and turn in my keys. I don't know what I'm going to do! I don't know how I'll tell my family. At my age, I can't find another job. I've got two children still in college. I need to see my pastor."

5

Losing a job usually involves more than loss of income. It involves loss of position, face, identity, opportunity, familiarity, and security that goes deeper than money. But few casseroles and cookies are delivered when a job loss causes grief. Because my deacon friend understood the necessity of grief work, he grieved his loss in time and then went on to find another job that, in his words, "made me glad I got fired in the first place." People have told me all the years of my pastorate, "As strange as it may sound, my life became better after this huge loss. But I had to work through my grief to discover this."

Moving Away from Your Place

My pastor friend called for help. "I've seen this new woman in our church several times. She is sad, listless, and hard to communicate with. I can't help her. Would you see her?"

After a few minutes in my office, I saw what he meant. I probed and listened intently and incessantly, what even seemed like eternally, but could get nowhere. Finally I thought to ask, "Have you lost anything important to you recently?"

"*Lost* anything?" she almost roared. "Let me tell you what I've lost!"

A few months earlier, her husband had called one afternoon to say, "I've got good news! I've been promoted, and my salary has almost been doubled. Oh, by the way, we will be moving to West Texas."

Six months prior to that phone call, this couple had moved into their dream house. They had saved for it for years. It had been designed by an architect friend and constructed by a contractor the woman had known all her life. They had spared no expense and the result was beyond their fondest fantasies. The house was next door to "Judy's" dearest friend, with whom she had walked to kindergarten the first day and shared all the intimacies of growing up. They lived on a beautiful cul-de-sac in suburban Connecticut and had coffee together every morning. They were best friends.

The day Judy and her husband arrived in our city—before airlines provided portable ramps from the plane and we had to brave the elements—the worst West Texas sandstorm anyone could remember blew all day. They moved into Holiday Inn, since there were no adequate houses available to rent or buy. It would take nearly a year for an unknown builder to get their new house ready. West Texas seemed so brown and flat and dry. "There are no trees here," Judy kept saying.

Her husband was busy and occupied every day. He was excited about his new challenges, authority, and income level. Judy was lonely and angry but did not want to ruin her husband's happiness. She said nothing to him or anyone else about what she was feeling. She felt betrayed, depressed, angry, and began considering divorce.

"Have I lost anything?" she wailed. "I've lost everything but 'Henry,' and he never comes home anymore. And when he does, he's too spent to relate to me. I'm dying!"

As Judy talked and I listened to her multiple losses, she began to come out of the shock and deprivation she felt. She told me she felt "great relief" just from having someone to talk to about her pain. She began rebuilding her life in a strange place. She began talking to Henry about her losses and her feelings. Talking through her grief went so well that when Henry got another promotion several years later and had the option to return to Connecticut, Judy wanted to stay in Lubbock. And they did!

To paraphrase Wayne Oates—unless we grow through grief, we never go through grief. Life *can* begin again after devastating loss. It can even be better.

Someone Leaving Home

When someone leaves home, grief usually occurs. He or she may be going to military service, which is layered with fear if the assignment is dangerous or life threatening. Or perhaps the person is going away to college, getting married, attending first grade, or even traveling to the barbershop for his or her first childhood haircut. The hair that goes into that little envelope is not the major loss. Instead, a mother says, "My last baby is growing up, and I can't stop crying." The loss may hit when a daughter leaves in a car with a boy for her first date or in your car once she has a driver's license.

Some people leave home in anger. Some depart a disrupted family system. Siblings sometimes do not speak to each other for decades, or parents are cut off from children because of family secrets or unresolved grievances. This occasions a deeper, more anxiety-ridden grief. Guilt may lurk as a hidden monster in the basement of our minds and hearts and come out at inopportune times in embarrassing or destructive ways.

A Disappointing Child

Repeatedly in my life and ministry, I have known and worked with parents who grieve the loss of their dream for a child. Sometimes children take the road of the irresponsible prodigal son—or the rigid elder brother—whom Jesus describes in Luke's fifteenth chapter. Whatever these parents do to try to help the child find his or her way, the child spurns their efforts and continues to disappoint them with gravely unacceptable behavior. One such parent said to me, "I hate this feeling, but in all honesty, I think my grief would be more possible to deal with if my child had been killed in an accident or died with a disease. She spurns our love and rejects our values, then comes home repentant and cooperative for a time, only to disappoint us again by living her life in a way that breaks our hearts. It's a grief that will not seem to go away."

A Violation of One's Self

All of us likely know people who have been robbed or burglarized or survived a fire, storm, or flood. Perhaps you have sustained such a loss yourself. In addition to losing tangible items and money, we lose irreplaceable items—pictures and other sacred symbols of the abiding values of our lives. Such things are worth little or nothing to a thief but are priceless to us.

Such loss can occasion a grief that erodes our sense of security and well-being. We are left feeling invaded, violated, angry, and even more vulnerable than we actually are to both criminal and random evil.

In another venue, several of my friends, parishioners, and counselees have had the horrific experience of being violated by rape. "Mary Jo" is an especially bright and beautiful student who had attended our church. After she went away to college, she spent the night with a sorority sister. Several students, male and female, were in and out of the apartment during the evening for a small party.

Late the next morning Mary Jo awoke in a stupor-like fog amid immense pain. She saw that her twin bed was covered and the room tracked with blood. Although she had gone to sleep alone and clothed, now her nude body had scratches and bruises in telling places. Her friend "Sally" was still in her own bed asleep —seemingly "dead to the world."

As they struggled to awaken, trying to piece together the meaning of this scene, they realized that a fellow partygoer, a young man they barely knew, had drugged them both. He admitted later that he had slipped a Rohypnol, GHB-type illegal pharmaceutical into each girl's glass. Mary Jo had been raped. She was so drugged that she still has no memory of the assault.

Although she is a stable person and an excellent student— highly intelligent, deeply spiritual, and assertive (her friends say "she has it together") she was devastated to the point of being dysfunctional. For months, aware that people do at times come apart emotionally due to being terrorized, she wandered in the horror of the awesome psychic pain the perpetrator left in his wake.

When I asked what she had lost, she said, "The main thing I guess is my childhood innocence that nothing like this would ever happen to me. I had always felt 'automatically safe' as though car wrecks and rapes happen to other people but not to me."

She spoke of beginning to question her trust in males, although she admitted, "I have been fortunate to be surrounded by strong, trustworthy men all my life."

She told me of her excruciating struggle with asking, "Was I in some way to blame? Did I contribute to what happened?" Having to grieve over and accept such all-consuming losses was almost overwhelming, she said, "for months and months."

When I asked if there were anything else she lost, she replied, "The losses were not just for me as an individual. Each member of my family had a major loss in his or her own way. They too felt violation, enormous rage, and helplessness."

She told me of her fearsome battle to regain her sense of security in the world. She had lost her virginity, plus her innocence and natural trust in the reliability of the universe as a safe place.

She also spoke of losing friends. Some people, she said, "can't seem to handle what happened to me." They seemed to have their own sense of a loss of safety plus a judgmental attitude. "I felt excommunicated from some circles," she said.

Such women have poured out their agony to me during all the years of my student and pastoral ministry. Many of them never spoke to anyone of the crime or their debilitating pain for years or even decades. I'm confident that many women have carried such agony to their graves.

Research as well as university administrators confirm that unbelievably large numbers of women are violated in similar ways every year. Through the cowardice of some predator who drugs them or overpowers them, not only their bodies but also their minds, hearts, and spirits, their very personalities—indeed their souls—are invaded and desecrated.

As Mary Jo spoke, I wondered if this boy had any idea that such drugs can be deadly if given in the wrong dosage or combined with an ethical pharmaceutical the woman is taking.

Molestation

Moreover, thousands of people abused as children by a trusted person (often a relative) carry their toxic secret and the attendant grief well into adulthood. They mourn, isolated and alone, mystified by why and how this kind of travesty could have ever happened to them.

"Jane" came to me as a counselee just as I was beginning the revision of this book. Her therapist had moved away, referring her to me. She wanted to complete the work she had begun, plus open discussion about her possible retirement.

She soon shared a sadness she had carried since preteen years. A family member had molested her and then admonished her, which is of course usual for such predators, not to "ever tell anyone."

When I invited her to say what she lost, she spoke quickly. "Power," she said. "I lost my power." And, although she is now a highly competent professional woman with graduate degrees, she said, "I felt quite powerless all my life until the day my counselor helped me find some freedom to tell her what had happened." Then she added, "He was older and stronger and there was nothing I could do. I was left with a confusion about life and my identity that still haunts me."

When I asked if there were anything else she'd like to say about this awful episode, she responded, "I would scream at the top of my lungs about what happened. I would let my parents know and I would cry from the depths of my being '*This is wrong!*'"

Then she volunteered, "We must tell young people that it's safe to tell an adult you trust. Tell them! You *must* take that risk for your own sake! How much of the grief which I have carried all these years would I have been spared had I summoned the courage to tell a trusted adult?"

Loss of Aim or Identity

"Joe" called me on Thanksgiving Day. "I apologize for calling today," he said, "but I've got to see you while I'm home from school. My life has fallen apart!"

Joe was a young church member and at that time a freshman at a small college. I had noticed he had not been home during the entire fall semester. The year before, his name was a household word in our town. He was one of the most outstanding ball carriers our football fans had ever seen. When he walked the halls of his high school or the streets of the town, people punched each other and said, "Wow! There's Joe! He's great!" He was a celebrity.

Joe was too small to be of interest to the scouts of the major colleges and too proud to settle for a scholarship at one of the many smaller schools that sought him. He decided to attend a college where he knew no one and could "just be a student."

"It's awful," he said when I asked him what he had lost. "No one knows me, no one cares. My life is over. I keep thinking of running my truck into a ditch. I'd come home and quit school, but I'm embarrassed." He talked, and I listened and asked questions and listened some more. We met again whenever he was home. I telephoned periodically and dropped by to see him when I traveled his way.

By chance, I talked to Joe a few weeks before writing this. He is now out of school, co-owner of a successful business, husband of a beautiful woman, and father of three bright children—one of whom is a "tiger" on the same high school gridiron. Now in mid-life, he told me of his gratitude for our pastoral conversations, and he spoke of his new aims and identity. "I can't believe I nearly ended it all and missed this," he said.

A Birth Defect, Surgery, or Illness

Birth defects, some kinds of surgery, chronic or debilitating illness, miscarriages, and many other medical ailments cause loss and, therefore, grief. My oldest cousin was born with Down Syndrome. He was the first grandson on that side of the family and named for our grandfather. The family had held great hopes for him. Even with his disability, he was a beautiful person—warm, fun, real, loving! But at the time of his death at age fifty-three, he could say only three words: "mama," "kitty," and "no." In our family system, we never talked about our pain. We tried to ignore it. All of us carried an unspoken grief we did not know how to address. How I wish we had known how to speak our pain so as to receive the comfort and encouragement that was available.

Rupture of a Friendship

Among the losses that bring grief is disruption of a friendship. I remember being overwhelmed by the request to present an older minister to the American Association of Pastoral Counselors for membership. He presented a written verbatim report of a counseling session and several taped interviews. The focus of his concern was a multiplicity of dreams his young parishioner was having. The young man was gravely depressed and considering suicide. All the joy had ebbed out of his life. My colleague gave great energy and time to interpreting these dreams since he was a graduate Jungian analyst, but at the end of his cover letter he questioned, "I am missing something here and I can't locate what it is. Could you make any suggestions?"

After digesting the verbatim and tapes my suggestion was this: Ask him if he has lost anything that caused him pain. Upon doing this, the minister called me with great excitement. "My young friend has made a breakthrough," he said excitedly. "Recently he was estranged from a dear friend with whom he knew I was acquainted. He didn't want to speak of this with me. But when I raised the question of loss, a dam seemed to break and he is now moving out of the cave of depression he's been living in."

Some of the deepest grief I have known has been due to a severed relationship. Something as traumatic as a major disagreement or as simple as a move may occasion a loss that we may not tend to associate with grief. Nevertheless, we grieve internally about the loss when we won't let it surface into our conscious minds and conversation.

Loss of a Dream or Opportunity

Many people grieve when time passes and they realize they will never have an opportunity they sought or even thought God had destined for them. My colleague in ministry commented years ago, "I was never just right for the jobs I wanted. I would hear the bishop say, 'You would be just right for that job if only you were a little older.' Then, all of a sudden, he began to say, 'You would really be right for that job if only you were a little younger.' I don't remember crossing the line!"

One day the reality may dawn that you will never be head of the department or manager or dean or president. Younger people are passing you by. Another version of this grief is that you *do* get to be CEO or dean or even President of the United States! Your dream comes true, your ship comes in, but you lack the power or prominence you envisioned, or the fulfillment is not as great as you imagined. Success feels barren. The halls are filled with Judas types who lurk, waiting for the critical moment to betray you.

Loss comes in many shapes and forms. With loss comes grief and the necessity of grief work, which is not unlike the labor of bearing a child. Failure, loss of face, embarrassment, losing your church or support group, loss of a relationship—so many losses occur as we journey through our pilgrimages.

In the movie *Whose Life Is It Anyway?* Richard Dreyfuss played Ken Harrison, a brilliant young sculptor who survived a horrible auto accident that resulted in his being a quadriplegic. In an instant, he lost the dream of becoming one of the world's great sculptors. Furthermore, he lost the capacity to have any control over his life and destiny. He could not even refuse an unwanted injection from his doctor who wanted to sedate him, dull his pain, and calm his panic.

The professionals assigned to Ken did not seem to want to hear his despair about his losses. They tried to distract him, humor him, give him pep talks, entertain him, and medicate him. No one ever asked the operative question: "Would you like to talk about your losses and how you feel about them?" No one was willing to listen!

I wish a scriptwriter had written a skillful, caring pastor—or even a Christian friend—into Ken Harrison's life. If someone had invited him to talk about his losses and feelings, just listening quietly; if someone in the story had learned something about the anatomy of grief and the gift of listening, Ken Harrison might have chosen to say good-bye to his grief and hello to a new life.

Notes

[1] Richard Ashley Rice, *The Best of Byron* (New York: Thomas Nelson and Sons, 1942), 73.

[2] Wayne E. Oates, *Pastoral Care and Counseling in Grief and Separation* (Philadelphia: Fortress Press, 1976), 78.

[3] Carl Whitaker, lecture at Texas Tech University, Lubbock TX, April 1985.

Chapter Two

Stages in the Journey toward New Life

G rief seems such an endless pain. So many people are hurting, yet they can move through grief if they will make the hard choice to face their pain. The wounds of grief can actually heal, though scars remain. Help, hope, peace, and new life are available if people choose to suffer, work, and grow through a crushing loss instead of staying in it.

"Evelyn" and I were friends in college. We had not kept up with each other, so I was surprised to see her at a widow's network meeting where I spoke on dealing with grief. I learned that she had returned home one day and found her forty-year-old husband dead of a heart attack. When I asked how she was coping with such a sudden and tragic loss, she said in a thin, overly melodic voice, "Just fine. I'm here to help the other people who aren't doing as well as I am." A little bell rang in my counselor's head: *I wonder how she's really doing?* But when I probed a bit, she demurred.

A few weeks later she called for an appointment. She had seen a doctor because of severe chest pains she was having. Her doctor had said, "Nothing is physically wrong with you, Evelyn. Your problem is that you haven't dealt with Sid's death. Go see a counselor. Ask for help with the grief you still carry." Six years had passed since that tragic afternoon when she found her husband dead on the floor.

The first few times we met, Evelyn could not use the word "dead." When I used it, she visibly flinched. She said, "I have a boulder the size of a large grapefruit in my chest. It won't go away. I do not want to go on living. I envy the nerve of my colleague who recently took her life."

After *significant* struggle and grief work, Evelyn was able to let go of her grief for Sid. Last January, I happened to see her in an airport on her way to a convention. She said, "Thank you for helping me face and work through my grief. I have married a wonderful guy whose wife died two years ago. We are happy. I am happy. God is here. Life is good. The boulder is gone!"

If we are to deal creatively and redemptively with the grief that comes with any significant loss, we must make a painful choice to work through a developmental process. Although counselors describe this process in various ways, I prefer the approach of Wayne Oates, who was acknowledged as an international authority regarding grief work. He said people tend to work through six stages of grief.[1]

(1) *Shock.* Major loss assaults us in such overpowering ways that we simply cannot accept it. We cannot quickly assimilate such an unwelcome and devastating reality. We may be stunned, as though we have had a physical blow to the head. We may be "in shock" or even act as though nothing serious has happened. We may seem "high" or even serene.

(2) *Numbness.* When shock begins to subside, we may "freeze up" or feel little or nothing. Such numbness is God's way of helping us assimilate unwelcome facts as quickly as possible. During this period of grief, we may feel that family, friends, or even God are distant and do not care about us and our pain. Food may taste bland or "funny." We may not care about people, things, or activ-

ities that formerly mattered. We are tempted to withdraw excessively from people and social occasions and then misperceive that they have withdrawn from us.

Thomas made this mistake after Jesus' resurrection. He withdrew from the fellowship of believers and went away to try to care for the emotional wounds he sustained at Jesus' death. Having withdrawn into himself, away from the others, he missed the appearance of Jesus that John described (see John 20). We, too, may withdraw into ourselves and miss the resurrection God wants for us. Of course, some solitude is necessary in facing grief. At times, though, we must push ourselves to be with people, particularly friends and the community of faith. Sometimes we must push ourselves to share deeper feelings with a trusted friend, pastor, or counselor.

(3) *Alternating between Fantasy and Reality.* At this stage of grief, we struggle continually between the reality of the unwelcome fact and the fantasy that "this is all a dream and the loss has not actually occurred." If we steel ourselves against the unwelcome reality, we usually experience an increase in destructive emotions. Anger, anxiety, guilt, depression, and/or cynicism may assault us so totally that we lose our ability to function normally, though we may not realize that we have done so. We may cling to or idolize our loss.

Some people remain in the fantasy phase and never recover. I know a woman in another state who still looks for the return of her son who died of cancer in 1959. When the phone rings, she thinks it is probably "Mike." His baseball cap is still on the four-poster bed where he hung it before the last trip to the hospital. This woman is frozen in the fantasy phase of grief. She idolizes Mike and idealizes his life. She has withdrawn permanently into her myth that he is still alive. If she faced the reality side of grief, however, a breakthrough perhaps could occur that is painful but productive of new life.

(4) *Flooding of Emotions and Grief.* At this stage, the wall between fantasy and reality breaks, and a flood of grief sweeps through and over us. We feel that nothing will ever be right again; we will never recover from this agony. We may lose all meaning in our lives, become bitter, hostile, vengeful, exceedingly weepy, or even feel that we are going crazy.

Take heart! To grieve is not to be crazy. This flooding of emotions and grief is a necessary step in working through grief. When we face the flooding, we take the necessary step that leads to new life. The reverse of what we fear will happen actually happens. The fear says, "If I ever start to cry, I'll cry forever." The reality is, "If I don't let my tears come into the open, my crying will never cease."

One of my parishioners faced the loss of his marriage, the loss of his children, the loss of his job, and then cancer. He said after he had worked through his grief and reestablished his life, "I now see that God gave me these tears to wash away my pain."

(5) *Selective Memory and Stabbing Pain.* After the outpouring of flooding grief, the grief process usually levels off to a more drawn out and less intense day-to-day reassociation of memories. A sight, a smell, or a song may elicit memories that bring a briefer, stabbing pain.

Daytime fantasies and bereavement dreams relieve anxiety. Guilt, anger, loneliness, and other emotions continue. But as one does the labor of grief work, light is seen at the end of a tunnel, reducing the feeling of being lost in a cave.

(6) *Acceptance of Loss/Reaffirmation of Life.* When we reach this final stage of grief, we have gone through our own death, burial, and resurrection regarding the loss. We experience a surprising reaffirmation of goals, values, and life itself. We are now capable of establishing new and meaningful relationships and reentering old ones with new enthusiasm. When we accept, grieve, and relinquish loss, we can enjoy life again. The God who created us in the

beginning and has walked with us "through the valley of shadows" can lead us into new life even after a massive, crushing loss.

Remember, experiencing grief is somewhat like labor pains! Grief work demands almost more from us than we can muster. To refuse to do grief work, however, is to be stuck in the valley of the shadow of death. When we become willing to let go, our resurrection becomes possible. C. S. Lewis said it well: "Nothing that has not died will be resurrected."[2]

New life was possible for the Old Testament character Samuel in his grief about the self-destruction of King Saul (see 1 Sam 16). Samuel discovered the possibility for Israel to have a new king and a new beginning. And the new king turned out to be a greater king than Saul. But Samuel had to act! When he moved into action in response to God's command, he chose the new life God wanted him to have. He had to turn loose of Saul to do so.

New life after grief is a treasure God wants to help us discover during our grief. Grief can be a bridge to a deeper life with God as creator, redeemer, and sustainer of life. When you are bereft by the agony of grief, God who lost a son wants to become your friend and companion in the journey of grief work and in the discovery of resurrection in a new life.

Notes

[1] Wayne E. Oates, *Pastoral Care and Counseling in Grief and Separation* (Philadelphia: Fortress Press, 1976), 79. See also Oates, *Anxiety in Christian Experience* (Philadelphia: Westminster Press), 51-56.

[2] C. S. Lewis, *The Weight of Glory*, cited in Reuben Job and Norman Shawchuck, *A Guide to Prayer for Ministers and Other Servants* (Nashville: The Upper Room), 185.

Chapter Three

Helping Each Other Grieve Creatively

O n September 19, 1978, Troy Organ, distinguished professor emeritus of philosophy at Ohio University in Athens, Ohio, lost his wife Lorena to suicide. Later, in an article for *The Christian Century*—"Grief and the Art of Consolation: A Personal Testimony"—he wrote:

> Consolation is indeed an art. It is the art of active love. Thanks to the consolation of those who listened, who touched, who invited me into their homes, who wept with me. I have found my way back to life. . . . I have received comfort from the Christian community, and I am indeed grateful to those who have sincerely tried to assist me in the very difficult task of dealing with the loss of a loved one through suicide. . . . As light displaces darkness, I recognize my debt to those who have been my comforters, and I pray that I have learned out of this experience both how to grieve and how to console.[1]

He informed my understanding of helping people in grief as much as anything I have ever read. "Grief is a helplessness that does not cry for help," he said. "One cries and hopes that help will come unbidden."[2]

In this chapter, I make a few suggestions about relating helpfully to people who have experienced a major loss.

Go

Be there! Offer the gift of your presence. Maya Angelou said it well:

> Lying, thinking
> Last night
> How to find my soul a home
> Where water is not thirsty
> And bread loaf is not stone.
> I came up with one thing
> And I don't believe I'm wrong
> That nobody,
> But nobody
> Can make it out here alone.[3]

People say, "I want to go, but I don't know what to say." My response to that is, "Good. That's better! Say nothing. Just go. If you must speak, say 'I'm sorry, I care,' and nothing else. Your presence will say everything that needs to be said." Most people say too much to grieving people anyway. People in grief are in such shock that they hear or remember basically nothing anybody says. Just go. If for some reason you cannot go, phone or write. Say "I'm sorry, I care, I love you. I'm here to help if I may." Remember that it is not necessary or even important to say anything. Indeed, it is crucial not to say too much at such a time.

Listen

Let the person in need of comfort talk. Let him or her talk about people, events, and feelings connected with the loss. One of the major tasks of grief is for the loss to become real. Going, being quiet, and *listening* will aid this process.

Listen particularly for feelings. Accept these feelings without judgment. Feelings are not moral or immoral, good or bad—they're just feelings!

I have been there many times as a pastor and have seen the scenario as people come to give the gift of their presence. I have heard the typical story:

> John has not been feeling well lately, but when he came in tonight he said he was feeling better. He ate such a good supper. His appetite seemed to be back. After supper he went in to listen to the news. I was puttering around the kitchen, finishing things. When I went in to join him, he seemed to be asleep in his chair. I tried not to disturb him, but then he seemed not to be moving at all. I spoke to him, then went over and touched him, and . . . he was gone!

Then the phone or the doorbell rings, and she tells the story all over again: "John hasn't been feeling well lately. But tonight he came in and had such a good supper. Then he went in to hear the news . . . ."

As caring people visit and call, she tells one of the most important stories of her life over and over again. Each time she repeats the story, the reality she is loathe to face sinks into her being a bit more. People who go and care and be a good enough friend to listen are crucially important.

Ask Questions

Ask brief, tactful questions. Ask about feelings, events, and people: "Do you want to talk about what happened?" "Would you be willing to tell me about your daughter?" "What is it like for you to be divorced?"

Troy Organ observed, "Friends poured in all afternoon. There were never less than a dozen people with me during the rest of the day. As each arrived, there was a brief expression of sorrow. Then conversation turned to the weather, politics, campus gossip. I wanted to talk about Lorena, but everyone else seemed to find this an embarrassing topic."[4]

No Preaching

Please don't interpret, explain, or offer premature hope! Troy Organ said, "It's cruel to say grief will end."[5] Don't argue with a person's feelings. The kindest, most helpful thing you can possibly do is simply to listen.

Touch

Appropriate touch—a hand on a shoulder, for example—offers a compassionate source of comfort. Don't be afraid to draw near to the grieving person.

Offer Specific Help

Don't say, "Call me if I can do anything." Instead, ask, "Could I pick anyone up at the airport for you?" "May I house some of the people coming from out of town?" "May I cut your lawn?" "May I pick you up for worship next Sunday?"

One of my parishioners said, "The best offer of help I had was from the person who said, "Maybe you are ready to return to worship but not ready to face a big crowd of people. Could I pick you up and get you there just as the service begins? Then we'll leave just as worship ends."

Troy Organ said the person who was the most help to him when his wife took her own life was the woman who said, "You are to be my guest every Thursday evening at 6:30 P.M. for supper. I have already set aside a napkin ring for you."[6]

People want to talk about their losses. They want us to listen to what they feel. We give them a priceless gift when we patiently listen to whatever they want to say. We neither judge nor argue. We forego telling "war stories" about our own losses and victories. We avoid telling people what to feel or how to face a loss. We don't explore why the tragedy happened. We listen.

My dear friends and fellow church members lost their teenage daughter and sister, Blair Smoak, in a tragic accident in 1992. In facing and seeking to work through their grief, they circulated an anonymous poem that invited people to speak with them about their darling Blair:

> The time of concern is over.
> No longer am I asked how my wife is doing.
> Too seldom is the name of our daughter
> > mentioned to me.
> A curtain descends. The moment has passed.
> A life slips from frequent recall.
> There are exceptions: close and compassionate
> > friends,
> Sensitive and loving family, Blair's closest pals.
> For most, the drama is over.
> The spotlight is off. Applause is silent.
> But for me the play will never end.
> The effects on me are timeless.
> Say Blair to me.
> On the stage of my life she will always be a rising
> > star!

Do not tiptoe around the most consuming event of
    my life.
Love does not die.
Her name is written on my life
Say Blair to me and say Blair again and again.
It hurts to bury her memory in silence—and I will
    not . . . .
So long as we are here, please say Blair to us.[7]

Notes

[1] Troy Organ, "Grief and the Art of Consolation: A Personal Testimony," *The Christian Century* (1–8 August 1979): 762.

[2] Ibid., 759.

[3] Maya Angelou, *Poems* (New York: Bantam Books, 1986), 69.

[4] Organ, "Grief and the Art of Consolation," 760.

[5] Ibid., 761.

[6] Ibid., 762.

[7] Anonymous, edited by Lewis and Betty Smoak.

Chapter Four

Saying Good-bye to Your Grief

Some people are not yet ready to say good-bye to grief. Others, much to their detriment, try to say good-bye to grief too quickly. Refusing to say good-bye to grief when it is time to do so, however, can be disastrous. Many people never say good-bye to grief and thus never say hello to life again after a crushing loss.

I invite you to say good-bye to grief at the appropriate time. God wants us to walk *through* the valley of the shadow of death—not walk to it and stay there. Both the Old and New Testaments teach that we are invited by God to move beyond grief.

In Matthew 5:4, Jesus says the single most important thing that has ever been said about grief. Eugene Peterson paraphrases it, "You're blessed when you feel you've lost what is most dear to you. Only then can you be embraced by the One most dear to you."[1] Today's English Version translates it this way: "Happy are those who mourn; God will comfort them!"

I hear Jesus saying three things in this sentence. First, mourning is both permissible and necessary for a believer. When we lose someone, we must grieve! We do grieve—openly or internally.

Second, we are blessed when we choose to mourn instead of trying to avoid the pain. Trying to avoid pain is always unsuccessful and actually prolongs and increases the pain. Third, when we grieve our losses, we can ultimately say good-bye to grief. We can walk through the valley of the shadow of loss and experience the state of well-being the Bible calls blessed. First Samuel 15:34–16:1 tells a story that provides important clues to how we may choose to deal with our grief:

> Then Samuel went to Ramah, and Saul went up to his house in Gibeah, and Samuel did not see Saul again until the day of his death. But Samuel grieved continuously over Saul and the LORD repented that he had made Saul king over Israel. So the LORD said to Samuel, "How long will you keep on grieving over Saul, seeing that I have rejected him from being king over Israel? Fill your horn with oil and go, and I will send you to Jesse, the Bethlehemite, for I have provided for myself among his sons a new king for Israel."

These few verses of Scripture offer three basic insights into the phenomenon we call grief. First, God blesses grief as a necessary reality when significant loss has occurred. It is natural, normal, and productive. God did not criticize Samuel for his grief over Saul. God did not say, "Samuel! Shame on you! You are a believer and you have no business grieving." Instead, God blessed Samuel's grief, shared his grief, and then commanded him to move through and beyond it. Second, grief is occasioned by losses other than death. Any significant loss occasions the need for grief. Samuel grieved over the moral and spiritual disintegration of the king of Israel. Third, at some point, God invites us, as he did Samuel, to say good-bye to grief and move on with the responsibilities and joys of living. God knows we cannot move on with life until we finish grieving and say good-bye to our loss.

God knows that some discoveries can be in our future if we are willing to grow into them.

Trying to take grief away from people is neither wise nor kind. When the time is appropriate to let grief go, it is necessary to do so. To turn grief over to God is to experience resurrection from grief, just as Jesus experienced resurrection from death— but only after he faced and experienced death!

Several years ago, I heard Fred Craddock talk about an experience at the time of his mother's death. Craddock is one of the most competent interpreters of Scripture in our world today. He taught New Testament interpretation and preaching at Candler School of Theology in Atlanta and still ministers now in his retirement. Craddock said that following his mother's death, a woman entered his home on the afternoon prior to the funeral carrying a large Bible. The woman emoted, "Isn't it great that your mother is now with the Lord? Isn't it wonderful that your mother is no longer here? She has been released from her suffering. You should all be so grateful!"

She said what most of us have felt after someone's long illness. When we make such statements to others, we are well-motivated and well-intentioned in trying to help. This lady, however—as sometimes people are prone to do—overstated her point and announced her feelings prematurely and intrusively. Craddock explained, I got up and addressed this woman: "Madam, I know that you mean well, and I know you do not intend to create a problem with us here by what you are saying. However, if you will read that Bible you are carrying around, you will notice that it does not simply say, 'He is risen.' It says, 'He is not here. He is risen.' The same thing is true of our mother. We know that our mother is in a better place. We know that our mother is free of her suffering. But please don't try to take our grief away from us. Please don't make us feel guilty about our pain. The truth is, we miss our mother."[2]

This episode encapsulates the two sides of the reality of saying good-bye to grief. First, Jesus did not get to the resurrection without going through the cross, and neither will we. He embraced rather than denied the pain. If we are to become able to participate in the renewal of life that is offered in the reality of the resurrection of Jesus Christ, we must experience our own garden of Gethsemane.

Second, like Samuel, we must decide to reestablish life after grief, even if we don't feel ready. Hope lies on both sides—in the cross and in the resurrection. Jesus got to the resurrection by going through the cross, death, burial, a tomb, tears, agony, loneliness, anger, frustration, and devastation. Jesus, like Samuel, embraced God's gift of new life in the fullness of time.

New life does not simply happen. Freedom from grief does not occur automatically. Contrary to cultural wisdom, time does not always heal all wounds. Wayne Oates said it well: "We don't just go through grief, we grow through it." Failure to grow in the process of grief causes some people never to reestablish their lives. They are unwilling to experience the pain and darkness of the tomb. Or they may be unwilling to embrace the opportunities God offers for new life.

Consider the following four actions or decisions to help you say good-bye to grief—to grow through grief so that you may move beyond it and be restored by God to newness of life.

Say Hello to Grief Work

To say good-bye to grief, begin by saying hello to grief work. The theorists who explain the process of grief in a major loss have chosen the word "work" to talk about the reality of grief. They speak of grief *work*.

You can never say good-bye to grief that you have not owned and internalized. It must be your grief. It must be allowed to surface. You must be allowed—by others and by yourself—to grieve, to mourn, to face and feel the pain.

First, to say hello to grief work, accept the pain of the loss. You cannot experience grief work without experiencing pain.

Our culture teaches avoidance and denial of pain. Non-acceptance of that pain means lack of grief work. Avoidance of that pain means denial and delay of the grief work and resurrection to a new life.

Second, allow and accept the comfort people offer, even though it is easy to deny that you have any pain or rationalize it away. My mother died in 1983. People came from the most surprising places to offer comfort. They came to me by letter and telephone and in person to say, "I am sorry about your mother. She was an important person to me. I want you to know that I share your sorrow at her death."

Everything in me wanted to explain away my pain in losing my mother: "She was past eighty years old. She had been ill for quite a long time. She had a long, productive life. She was ready to go, and really it is a good thing that she could. Her death was a release for her, for my father, and for me."

Of course, all of that was true. But if I focused on that release too soon and dodged the reality that it was painful to lose someone I loved, then I would have missed the grief work as well as the resurrection that awaited me on the other side of grief.

Third, to say hello to grief work, keep reviewing the loss. Remember, rehearse, talk about, and feel positive and negative feelings. Don't hesitate to tell the stories of your loss and pain, your joys and treasured memories, again and again. Struggle, as James Fowler said, to "gradually bring the lived story of our lives into congruence with the core story of the Christian faith."[3]

Fourth, accept the many fears that come with grief: "Who else am I going to lose? What else is going to happen? Bad things happen in threes." (I have never been able to find that verse in the Bible, but many people are convinced that it exists.) You may have fears of being overwhelmed ("If I ever start crying I will never be able to stop") or of going insane; these fears must be accepted and expressed.

Fifth, exercise the freedom to express sorrow, the sense of loss, guilt, anger, or agony. Allow the grief to surface; do not keep it hidden inside your personality. Pour out your feelings as a part of the grief work.

Sixth, be aware that you are constantly moving in a struggle between the various stages of grief until God gives a reaffirmation of life. The stages of grief do not occur in a simple or well-structured manner, so do not simply go through them; *grow* through them.

Finally, say good-bye to *your* grief—not grief in general or pain in general. Say good-bye to grief that you have owned and internalized. Feel the pain—your own pain, your own loss, your own agony of mourning. As painful as it may be, it is indeed possible to cut yourself loose from your loss, as Samuel did, and proceed with claiming a new life.

Say Good-bye to Your Loss

To say good-bye to grief, say good-bye to loss.

Grady Nutt, the great humorist and TV star, was a good friend from my teenage years. Several years ago he called me and said, "I want to tell you a great story." Grady was one of the great storytellers. He called frequently with a funny story, so I fastened my seat belt. This story was not funny, however. It was profound. I am so glad I heard it before I had to face Grady's death—and my own grief about his death.

He said,

> A pastor I know was talking to a funeral director friend of his in Texas yesterday. For years he has been one of the most effective funeral directors in the Dallas area.
>
> Recently he learned that he had terminal cancer and only had a short period of time to live. This courageous man called his whole family together in the den of his home and sat them down. "I want to tell you something," he said. "I have learned that I

have terminal cancer. I do not have long to live. I have watched people from the vantage point of the funeral profession all my life. I have helped people bury their dead for decades, and I want to tell the people who are dearest to me in all the world something extremely important. Listen to me carefully: When I die, bury me. If you won't let me die, I will never let you live."[4]

I wrote down the advice and memorized it. Grady, not knowing he was less than a month away from his own death, gathered his family together and told them this story. The advice is not easy to take, but to say good-bye to grief, you must relinquish your loss—let go of the person you loved.[5]

I had that experience when Grady died. Seldom in my lifetime have I been so assaulted by a loss and so devastated by grief as I was when he was so tragically and suddenly killed. I answered the phone at 2:18 A.M. and heard my good friend Mark Bass say, "I have bad news. Grady is dead."

"Dead?!"

"Killed in an airplane crash!"

I thought, *There is some mistake. That cannot be. I was with him in San Antonio last week.* I went through everything we go through when a death occurs. I was in agony immediately and continuously. I was in denial and shock. I could not believe it!

After struggling with my grief for a long while, I had a dream. I was on a tower that seemed to be higher than the highest airplane from which I have ever viewed the earth. I could look down and see fields beneath me. They seemed about 80,000 feet below. The platform on this tower was about the size of a boxing ring. It had a thin, rickety picket fence around it.

While I stood and looked from the platform I thought, *Man, if I fell off this thing, I would fall forever. This is not a safe place to be. I need to get down.*

Suddenly, Grady appeared! He was bopping around, dancing like Snoopy does in the comics and on television—just dancing

35

around, celebrating life, and having a wonderful time. I was thinking, *That crazy guy needs to be careful or he is going to fall off this thing.*

About that time he spun around, backed into that little picket fence, and fell through it. I rushed over to the side and watched for what seemed an eternity in my dream. He fell and fell and fell and fell. There is no way I can describe to you the agony I felt in the dream as he fell.

After what seemed an eternity, I saw a huge cloud. Smaller clouds shaped like strong, muscular arms reached out and caught Grady. Then these giant arms enfolded him into a big hug. I woke up and felt a sense of peace.

On one hand, the pain was still there; on the other hand, I had let go of the person I lost. I knew I had seen God's arms. I learned again that if I am ever going to say good-bye to grief, I have to relinquish the loss. I have to accept the reality that the person is gone and will not be back.

To say good-bye to grief, accept the loss and relinquish the person or thing you have lost.

Say Hello to God

A third step seems to be foundational: saying hello to God. First I invited you to say hello to grief work. Then I invited you to say good-bye to your loss. Now I invite you to say hello to God.

Many people would be critical of hearing a minister say as much as I have said without mentioning the necessity of turning to God with your grief. However, I have had enough experience with my own grief and that of other people to know that unless you are ready to say hello to God, it is too early to try to do so. Sometimes we humans can be so mad at God that we just can't say hello. As we see in Psalms, such anger is acceptable.

At some point, grief sufferers are likely able to affirm with the great psalmist, "When I walk through the valley of the shadow of death, I will fear no evil, for thou art with me." We are able to quit talking about God and start talking to God: "Thou art with me." But it may take a while to be ready to let God have our grief.

I have learned that when I can say hello to God, it helps me say good-bye to grief. I may not be able to say hello to God until I have done some grief work, however.

Wayne Oates has said, "The assunderness of life is not healed by nostalgia."[6] I would add that it is also not healed by time, keeping busy, or any of the other bromides our culture recommends. Oates continues, "The assunderness of life is healed by translating our terror of the future into reverence for God."[7] To say good-bye to grief, we must say hello to the God who wants resurrection to happen again—this time in our lives.

Saying hello to God is what I believe my dream helped me do following Grady's death. It helped me know what my pain had caused me to forget: God loves Grady more than I. Grady has experienced his own resurrection, his own homecoming, and that eternally deep well-being the Scriptures call *shalom*. I must leave him with God and move ahead into my future.

Say Hello to Your Future

Finally, to say good-bye to grief, say hello to your future as God's gift of resurrected life. God gives the gift of resurrection and enables you to say hello to the future.

This hope for saying hello to God can be offered too early, too strongly, or too glibly. But it is hope that the resurrection that occurred following the loss of God's only begotten son is a resurrection that can happen again after we grieve a loss.

Harvey Cox, the Harvard theologian, once said, "In grief we are caught between nostalgia on one hand and fear of the future on the other. Fearing the future, we shrink back into nostalgia."[8] He points to the grim reality that we can get stuck in our grief if we love nostalgia and fear the future.

I remind you of Oates's saying, "The assunderness of life is healed not by nostalgia but by translating our terror of the future into reverence for God and faith in God." We cannot heal ourselves. God is the one who can give us life anew.

My colleague John Claypool and I shared the death of Grady Nutt. He and I were serving on the pastoral team of Second Baptist Church in Lubbock, Texas, when Grady was killed. John had been Grady's dear friend and pastor in Louisville, Kentucky. Grady had been with us for a four-day emphasis in our congregation three weeks before his death. As we struggled with the tragedy of Grady's death, John told me of an experience he had at Laity Lodge shortly before coming to Lubbock. He said this experience helped him let go of the loss of his daughter and move on in his new life without her.

John's eight-and-a-half-year-old daughter, Laura Lue, was diagnosed with acute leukemia. Eighteen months and ten days later, she died. One night about twelve years later, when Laura Lue would have been twenty-three, John spoke at Laity Lodge in the wilds of southwest Texas. The next morning he went to breakfast. A lady he had not met the evening before came up to him and said, "Dr. Claypool, I need to talk with you." He could tell from the look in her eyes that she was deeply serious. She said, "I had an experience last night and I do not know what to do about it, but I feel I must share it with you, though I am hesitant to do so."

He said, "Please go ahead. I am eager to help if I may." She told this story:

> I had a dream last night. I dreamed that I was in England at Oxford University in the library. I was walking through the library trying to be quiet, trying not to disturb anyone, when I saw a beautiful blonde-haired woman in her early twenties sitting at a desk. As I looked at her, I thought, "What a beautiful young woman she is. I wonder what she is preparing herself for?"

She motioned to me, and I went over to her. The young woman said, "My name is Dr. Claypool, and I understand that you know my father."

I said, "That is not exactly true. I really don't know your father. I have heard him speak and I know of him, but we are not friends, even acquaintances."

The young woman rushed right past that and said, "I wonder if you would be willing to take my father a message?"

I said, "Yes, I suppose I would."

She said, "Tell my father that I am here at Oxford working in leukemia research, and I am right on the edge of a breakthrough that will help people be able to recover from this dreaded, terminal illness. We get right to the edge of being able to make the discovery we are so eager to make, and then it falls apart in our hands. We have to back off, regroup, and begin again. We get there and we lose it, and we get there and we lose it. I have become convinced that the reason we cannot make this breakthrough is that my father won't let me go. Would you please, the next time you see my father, ask him to turn me loose? Ask him: 'Will you please let me go on with my life and you go on with yours?'"[9]

John said, "It helped. It helped me to do what I had been trying without success to do since the day of her death. The woman's dream was a gift of God to me that allowed me to let Laura Lue go."[10]

Brian Wren's resurrection hymn helps me hear a word from God:

> When grief is raw and music goes unheard,
>   and thought is numb,
> We have no polished phrases to recite.
> You are our Lord, in faith we grasp familiar words:
>   "I am the resurrection. I am life."

When time gives room for gratitude and tears,
Lord, make us free to grieve, remember, honor, and
    delight.
Let love be strong to bear regrets and banish fears.
    "I am the resurrection. I am life."
The height and breadth of what your love
    prepares
Soar out of time beyond our speculation and our
    sight.
The cross remains to earth the promise that it bears.
    "I am the resurrection. I am life."
All shall be judged, the greatest and the least, and all
    be loved,
Till every heart is healed, all wrong set right.
Sing and be glad, the Lamb prepares his wedding
    feast,
And in the midst of death, we are in life.[11]

It is possible to say good-bye to your grief. It is, to quote the Apostle Paul, conceivable that "the same divine energy which was demonstrated in Christ when God raised him from the dead"[12] can become available to you as God leads you to new life. Amid the wreckage of whatever loss still binds you to the past, you can grow through it to the genesis of new life. If you are ready to say good-bye to your grief and if you need to say hello to your future, I pray that you will choose to do so.

I invite you: Say hello to grief work. Say good-bye to your loss. Say hello to God. Say hello to your future. As you do, you will say good-bye to your grief and move into new life and new joy. I wish you God speed.

Notes

[1] Eugene Peterson, *The Message* (Colorado Springs: NavPress, 1993).

[2] Sermon at Alamo Heights United Methodist Church, San Antonio, Texas.

[3] James Fowler, *Becoming Adult, Becoming Christian: Adult Development and Christian Faith* (San Francisco: Harper & Row, 1984), 140; also see chs. 4 and 5.

[4] Wayne E. Oates, *Pastoral Care and Counseling in Grief and Separation* (Philadelphia: Fortress Press, 1976), 79.

[5] Telephone conversation with Grady Nutt, October 1982.

[6] Oates, *Pastoral Care and Counseling,* 79.

[7] Ibid., 78.

[8] Ibid., 79.

[9] With permission of John Claypool.

[10] Ibid.

[11] Brian Wren, *Faith Looking Forward* (Carol Stream IL: Hope Publishing, 1983), 32.

[12] J. B. Phillips, *Letters to Young Churches: The Letter to Ephesus,* cf. Ephesians 1:19-20 (New York: MacMillan Co., 1947), 106.

Chapter Five

How Long Does It Take to Grieve?

E arly in my life I thought that real Christians do not grieve. I thought if one believed in God and had a living relationship, he or she was exempt from grief and the pain of loss like a bright student from an exam. When I started reading the Bible and the literature of grief, I realized that we all grieve when we lose something or someone valuable. The difference in Christians and others is, to quote Paul the apostle, that Christians do not grieve "as those who have no hope" (1 Thess 4:13, TEV).

Christians work through their grief with the companionship of Jesus the Christ who suffered and died, "a man of sorrows, acquainted with grief." Christians are given the encouragement and strength of God who lost his only son. God as Father, Son, and Spirit shares our grief and helps us work through and beyond our sorrows. As Brian Wren's great hymn invites us to sing, "If faith comes true and Jesus lives, there'll be an end to grieving!"[1]

But how long does it take to come to this end of grieving? People ask me frequently, "Pastor, how long will this awful grief last?" I mentioned earlier my friend "Evelyn" who, six years after her husband's untimely death, still could not utter the word "dead." She said again and again as we mourned her loss, "This agony will never end. This grapefruit-sized stone in my chest will never go away. My life is over!" Yet, through redemptive grief work, she learned that her life was not over. In the power of God, it began again—to the point that she expressed true joy to me about her recovery and new life.

How long does it take to grieve?

In one sense, grief lasts forever. We must face the fact that when major loss occurs, we will always remember the person or the "something" that was lost, and when we remember painful loss, we naturally feel pain. Pain is a gift of God without which we would be impoverished.

In another sense, however, grief does end and new life can begin. This new life occurs on the other side of grief work when we have walked "*through* the valley of the shadow of death."

Samuel learned about the end of grief and the beginning of new life from Yahweh at Ramah. Samuel learned that God wants a spiritual statute of limitations on our grief so that, at some point, we may go on with our lives in the recovery of strength and joy even though we continue to remember our loss. God did not criticize Samuel for grieving. Rather, God invited Samuel to lay aside his grief and move on into the exciting and valid discovery of a new king for Israel: "How long will you go on grieving over Saul? I have rejected him from being king over Israel. Now, get some olive oil and go to Bethlehem to a man named Jesse. I have chosen one of his sons to be king" (1 Sam 16:1, TEV).

I hear God saying to Samuel, "Get your ordaining kit and go! Your grief has imprisoned you long enough. It's time to go on with your life. It's time to pick up a new challenge and responsibility." God invited Samuel to move beyond the threatening events of King Saul's demise into a new level of security and well-being in the development of God's new plan for Israel. We can learn from this.

It was not that Samuel did not have a genuine loss to grieve or that God was unsympathetic with Samuel's taking an appropriate time to grieve. Saul had been a great king. He was tall, mighty, and powerful. He won victories and established control. And he was religious! He believed the right "believables." He sacrificed correctly in the religious observances. His attitude and behavior were the problems. He was disobedient to Yahweh, so God rejected him as king (see 1 Sam 15:22-23).

Samuel grieved this loss in a prolonged agony. "As long as he lived he never again saw the king; but he grieved over him" (1 Sam 15:34, TEV). Samuel felt betrayed. The object and idea of his devotion were falling apart. He was angry, discouraged, empty, and in pain. Saul had led the people away from God in the name of doing the work of God. Samuel was disappointed. He grieved mightily over what Saul had done to himself and the people of Israel. God was sympathetic to Samuel. God grieved, too, but God was more invested in renewal than loss. God focused on moving on with life into the creativity and fullness of a new day. God wanted to help Samuel grow through and beyond his grief.

Monica McGoldrick has helped me with my grief and my attempts to invite others to grieve and then move on. She writes, "The primary goal of therapeutic intervention around death (or any other loss) is to empower and strengthen families to mourn their losses and move on."[2]

McGoldrick suggests four answers to the question, *How long will it take to grieve this loss?* She says it takes long enough to:

(1) Share the acknowledgement of the reality of the loss.
(2) Share the experience of the loss and put it into context with the rest of your life.
(3) Reorganize your family or personal system and make the necessary shifts in critical roles.
(4) Reinvest in other relationships and life pursuits.

As noted in chapter 2, Wayne Oates suggests that it takes long enough to work through the levels of shock, numbness, alternating between fantasy that the loss has not occurred and the reality that it has, the flooding of thoughts and emotions, selective memory and stabbing pain, and, finally, the acceptance of the loss and the reestablishment of life.[3]

Both McGoldrick and Oates offer hope that grief will end and new life will begin. Steps 1 and 2 in Oates' construct are similar to step 1 in McGoldrick's. Through shock and numbness we struggle to acknowledge the reality of loss. Oates's alternating and flooding stages of correspond to McGoldrick's calling for sharing the experience of the loss and putting it into context.

The play and movie *Steel Magnolias* has a touching example of how differently some people deal with the same loss. In the story, M'lynn is the mother (played by Sally Fields) of a beautiful daughter, Shelby (played by Julia Roberts). Shelby is diabetic and needs a kidney transplant. M'lynn decides to donate the necessary kidney, but Shelby's body rejects the kidney. She is put on life support systems. After an agonizing period of time, the family decides that the merciful choice is to unplug the respirator that prolongs Shelby's death but not her life. After the graveside service, M'lynn continues her grief work with her network of female friends—the "Steel Magnolias." "They turned off the machines," M'lynn says. "Drum [M'lynn's husband] left. He couldn't take it. Jackson [Shelby's husband] left. It's sort of amusing in a way. Men are supposed to be made of steel or something. I just sat there. I held Shelby's hand. There was no noise, no tremble. Just peace. O God! I realize how *lucky* I am! I was there when that wonderful creature drifted into my life, and I was there when she drifted out. It was the most precious moment of my life."[4]

This powerful scene in the movie is an example of how a mother and her network of friends struggle to put such an unwelcome death into the larger context of life. M'lynn's sense of privilege and giftedness at being there when Shelby's life began and when it ended, as agonizing as it was for her, gives meaning to her life and pain. Even as she leaves the graveside in abject agony about the loss of her daughter, she already focuses on the total context of gift and not only the agony of her loss or that final experience of death.

The viewer is left with the notion that M'lynn and these other "Steel Magnolias" are going to rise to the occasion, reorganize the expanded family system, and move on with life even amid such excruciating loss and pain.

The movie helped me focus on what Samuel learned in visiting Jesse's household: grief begins to end when one accepts the loss, focuses on God who gives the gift of life, and then moves on into the realization that resurrection of meaning and joy do follow the laborious work of grief.

In an earlier scene of *Steel Magnolias*, Shelby gives articulate testimony to the quality she wants in her life and the way she feels about risking death to have a child. Her mother tries to convince her to take the cautious path and not have children to avoid the toll on her already frail body. Shelby wants her mother to see that how long her life lasts is not as important to her as how fully she lives. She says, "Momma, I'd rather have thirty minutes of wonderful than a whole lifetime of nothin' special."

The closing scene in *Steel Magnolias* furnishes an excellent framework for getting grief work started. We see tears, anger, tenderness, concern, unreadiness to be religious, laughter, gallows humor—all the stuff of which grief and grief work are made. We see the importance of friends being with each other as loss happens and grief work begins. This is one of the most poignant scenes in film concerning how grief expresses itself in cataclysmic changes of emotional direction.

After the funeral is over and the crowd leaves the graveside, M'lynn stands at the casket alone. One of her friends approaches.

> Friend: How you holdin' up, honey?
> M'lynn: Fine.
> Friend: It was a beautiful service. The flowers were the
>   most beautiful I have ever seen.

M'lynn: They were beautiful.

Annelle *(immature religious stereotype)*: Miss M'Lynn, it should make you feel better that Shelby is with her king.

M'lynn: Yes, Annelle, I guess it should.

Annelle: We should all be rejoicing!

M'lynn: *(irritated)*: You go on ahead. I'm sorry if I don't feel like it. I guess I'm a little selfish. I'd rather have her here.

Annelle: Miss M'lynn, I don't mean to upset you by sayin' that. It's just that when something like this happens, I pray very hard to make heads or tails of it. And, I think that in Shelby's case, she just wanted to take care of that little baby and of you, and of everybody she knew. And her poor little body was just worn out. It just wouldn't let her do all the things she wanted to—so she went on to a place where she could be a guardian angel. She will always be young. She will always be beautiful. And I personally feel much safer knowing that she is up there on my side. It may sound real simple and stupid, and maybe I am—but that's how I get through things like this.

M'lynn: I 'preciate that. And it's a real good idea. Shelby, as you know, wouldn't want us to get mired down and wallow in all this. She would want us to handle it the best way we know how and get on with it. That's what my mind says. I just wish somebody'd explain it to my heart! *(tears)*

Another friend: Oh, honey, are you okay?

M'lynn: I'm fine. I'm *fine*! I can jog all the way to Texas and back, and my daughter never could. I'm so mad I don't know what to do. I want to know why! I want to know why Shelby's life is over. I want to know how that baby will ever know how wonderful his mother was, what she went through for him. No. No. No! *No*!! It's not supposed to happen this way! I'm supposed to go first! I've always been ready to go first. I don't think I can take this! I don't think I can take this! I just want to hit somebody 'til they feel as bad as I do. I just want to hit something. I want to hit it hard!

Friend: Here! Hit this. *(The friend grabs Ouisa, the stereotypical heavyweight of the movie, and pulls her into place for M'lynn to hit.)* Go ahead, M'lynn. Hit her hard. We'll make a T-shirt: "I slapped Ouisa Boudreaux." Hit her! Ouisa! This is your chance to do something for your fellow man. M'lynn, knock her lights out.

Friend: M'lynn, you just missed the chance of a lifetime. Everyone in Chickapin parish would give their eyeteeth to take a whack at Ouisa!

Ouisa *(to friend)*: You are a pig from hell.

The agony, the anger, the questions, the religious speeches, the urge to hurt someone, the gallows humor all illustrate the kaleidoscope of feelings that assault us when we lose someone or something we love dearly.

This scene in the movie points to the necessity of expressing our feelings—whatever they are. Such expression of feelings begins the grief process and moves us in a direction of healing and wholeness. If such feelings are denied or bottled up, they go underground and find expression in less healthy, destructive ways. Grief work can never be completed until it begins.

Grief work can never begin until we are willing to start at an unskilled, uncomfortable level. We must get started, even though we feel foolish in the process and even though we feel uncertain about how to proceed.

Everything I was taught as a child about expressing and not expressing feelings gets in my way when I must grieve. Everything in me says, "Big boys don't cry! Nice boys don't get mad! If you can't say something positive, don't say anything at all.

Real athletes play hurt and ignore their pain. The show must go on."

While these thoughts may have some validity in our lives, they do not apply to grief and the labor of grief. I have learned that to do something skillfully and appropriately I first must do it unskillfully and uncomfortably. I have learned that the ancient cultures that wore black armbands and observed periods of mourning and recovery after massive loss had a wisdom we would do well to emulate. If I do not face my grief and work through it and grow through it, I will grieve longer than necessary and never go on with my life. If I won't let my loss die, it will not let me live. If I stay in love with my loss or my grief, my love becomes a sarcophagus. If I mourn my loss, embrace my pain, and follow the one who is "a man of sorrows, acquainted with grief," life can become whole and new again.

M'lynn was right. "We've just got to do the best we can."

So how long does it take to grieve?

(1) Long enough to focus on the gift rather than the loss.
(2) Long enough to face the loss and put it into context with the rest of your life.
(3) Long enough to follow the leadership of God into the discovery of new life—which may in some ways be even better than the old one.
(4) Long enough to respond to new challenges of sharing grace with others in the agonies of their grief.

Grief begins to end when we can focus on the gift. While the loss never ebbs completely, the gift can transcend the loss and furnish a new impetus to accept the challenge of going on with life. It is not easy to focus on the gift, but it can happen.

John Claypool told an instructive story at the conclusion of his sermon "Life is Gift," following the death of his daughter, Laura Lue. While he was growing up, John's family had no washing machine. When an associate of John's father was drafted in

World War II, he suggested that the Claypools use his washing machine while he was away. John said, "So this is what we did, and it helped us a great deal."[5] He added:

> But eventually the war ended, and our friends returned; in the meantime I had forgotten how the machine had come to be in our basement in the first place. When they came and took it, I was terribly upset, and I said so quite openly.
>
> My mother, being the wise woman she is, sat me down and put things in perspective for me: "Wait a minute, son. You must remember, that machine never belonged to us in the first place. That we ever got to use it at all was a gift. So, instead of being mad at its being taken away, let's use this occasion to be grateful that we had it at all."[6]

Then Claypool added his own salient wisdom concerning Laura Lue's death even amid the pain and agony of losing his precious child:

> Here, in a nutshell, is what it means to understand something as a gift and to handle it with gratitude, a perspective biblical religion puts around all of life. And I am here to testify that this is the only way down from the mountain of loss. I do not mean to say that such a perspective makes things easy, for it does not. But, at least it makes things bearable when I remember that Laura Lue was a gift, pure and simple, something I neither earned nor deserved nor had a right to. And when I remember that the appropriate response to a gift, even when it is taken away, is gratitude, then I am better able to try and thank God that I was ever given her in the first place.[7]

He then gave this invitation to the congregation: "Will you join me in trying to learn to travel this way?"[8] I know that my friend John still feels pain about his beloved Laura Lue and always will. I also know that he travels the roadway of gratitude as his avenue of life. He has become a wounded healer to many others and to me. He has been a steward of his suffering and wisdom. He has used "the clay of his suffering to make a healing balm"[9] and has shared it with us in our agony.

When my wife Ardelle struggled with what we thought could be a terminal malignancy in 1976, when Grady Nutt's death devastated me in 1982, when my mother's death left me in shock in 1983, John was more than my colleague and partner in ministry. He was more than my friend. He was my minister and teacher concerning the life that is a gift of God.

He helped me say hello to grief work, good-bye to my losses, and hello to God and God's gracious gifts. Most of all, he helped me focus on life as a precious, priceless gift from God. He helped me focus on what I had been given more than on what I had lost. In doing so, thank God, John helped me say hello to my future.

How long does it take to grieve? Long enough to focus on the gift more than the loss. Long enough to trust God who is giver of all gifts with the well-being of yourself and your future. Long enough to decide to go on with the priceless gift of life, grateful for what you lost and hopeful in your new beginning!

Notes

[1] Brian Wren, *Faith Looking Forward* (Carol Stream IL: Hope Publishing Co., 1983), 31.

[2] Monica McGoldrick, "Echoes from the Past: Helping Families Mourn Their Losses," in *Living Beyond Loss: Death in the Family*, ed. Monica McGoldrick and Froma Walsh (New York: W. W. Norton and Co., 1991), 54-55.

[3] Wayne E. Oates, *Anxiety in Religious Experience* (Philadelphia: Westminster Press), 51-56.

[4] *Steel Magnolias*, produced by Ray Stark and directed by Herbert Ross, 118 minutes (Tri-Star Pictures, 1990), videocassette. Transcription by author.

[5] John Claypool, *Tracks of a Fellow Struggler* (Waco: Word, Inc., 1974), 81.

[6] Ibid.

[7] Ibid., 81-82.

[8] Ibid., 82-83.

[9] Carlyle Marney, *These Things Remain* (Nashville: AbingdonCokesbury, 1953), 60.

Chapter Six

Saying Hello to Your Life After Grief

We have just considered how long it may take for grief to end. The quote from British hymnologist Brian Wren that "there'll be an end to grieving" seems to requires further attention as we consider saying hello to a new life after grief.

In 1979 Wren was asked to compose a hymn for the funeral of his uncle, who was not a believer. He wrote a hymn that underlines the hope of resurrection and points to the promise of a genuine, joyous life that includes "wonders far more strange . . ." Let's look at the entire text:

> Let hope and sorrow now unite
> To consecrate life's ending,
> And praise good friends now gone from sight
> Tho' grief and loss are rending.
> The story in a well loved face,
> The years and days our thoughts retrace
> Are treasures worth defending.

With faith or doubt or open mind
 We whisper life's great question.
The ebb and flow of space and time
 Surpass our small perception;
Yet knowledge grows with joyful gains
 And finds out wonders far more strange
Than hope of resurrection.

Be glad for life in age or youth.
 It's worth is past conceiving.
And stand by justice, love and truth
 As patterns for believing.
Give thanks for all each person gives.
 If faith comes true and Jesus lives,
There'll be an end to grieving.

If there is "an end to grieving" and there is the hope of finding "joy and wonders far more strange than hope of resurrection," as Wren suggests in his second stanza, it is worth the cost for us to pay attention to moving toward a new life following grief. We can, with God's help, "be glad for life" even after a devastating loss.

The idea that in one sense some grief never ends is worth repeating. This is true in the sense that one never forgets the loss or its value. One always remembers with nostalgia and perhaps pain that there was a day when what was lost was a beloved life-giving part of one's existence. This memory will likely never completely fade. Nor does it need to.

However, as we saw with Samuel and King Saul, God was able to lead Samuel and the nation Israel beyond the grim tragedies of Saul into a new life with King David. In this case, the later life was indeed more fulfilling than the former, although this could not have even been imagined too early in the development of the scenario. David was, to be sure, an unlikely candidate to replace the mighty King Saul! Maybe we need to be willing to consider unlikely paths to release us from our bondage.

If David could follow Saul and resurrection Sundays can follow the tragic loss of crucifixion Fridays, could it be that hope and new life also await you on the other side of your grief? The following are steps that can help lead you to the other side of grief.

Learn to Grieve

We are more likely to say hello to a life after grief when we are willing to grieve in an unskilled way. My friend Tom Cloer, senior professor of education and reading at Furman University, has given a speech focused on the statement that "anything worth doing is worth doing badly." My English teacher mother would be aghast at that statement. She tried her best to teach me that "anything worth doing is worth doing *well*." That is certainly true, but Tom also has a valid point. To learn to do something well, one usually has to go through a time of doing it less than well. I am convinced that this is one thing that delayed me in learning to express my grief. Afraid that I could not do it well, I didn't do it at all. Afraid of being embarrassed, I was hesitant to step out and risk sharing my true feelings. If I had been willing "to do it badly," I believe I would not have been stuck for such a long time.

As a high school student, I learned to play an instrument in the band. My first fledgling attempts were dissonant and wobbly to say the least, even to my own ears. I cannot imagine how bad my playing sounded to others. But in time, with an excellent coach and with faithful practice, I was promoted to first chair in a division 1 award-winning high school band. Later I loved being part of a superior university band for another four years. I began by doing badly and I learned to do well. Fulfillment followed!

Actually, my interest in band grew from one of my early losses. It was a painful episode that I did not recognize as grief. My father accepted a new job following my freshman year in high school. In Texas, one was by definition ineligible to play sports for a full year after moving from one school district to another. I was devastated that I could not play football during fall season. I had lettered in my freshman year and was convinced that I would start and—in my fantasy—probably star the next year. But because of the move, I couldn't even suit up for the games; I was ruled out on a technicality. What a loss! In addition to the sports loss, I had left my first "true love" behind, and I was certain I would never find anyone as wonderful as she. To top that off, my face broke out into the worst case of teenage acne ever. I felt like I was being punished for something. I thought my life was over! Soon, though, after joining the band, meeting friends who were willing to welcome me, and falling for a new girlfriend, I learned that I could live and enjoy life after loss.

In the big picture of life, these are small, easily healed teenage losses. But at the time, they were grim and serious to me! Yet as I adjusted to my loss and sought new interests, I was amazed that I also found new life. This teen experience has served as a paradigm of hope for me in subsequent, more serious losses when I thought life would never be as good again. As a sophomore in a new place, I grieved. I was in pain and despair. I made a few trips back to the former town trying to recapture the magic I felt as a freshman in high school. But the hope that life would be good again became reality for me only when I decided to move on and choose to risk plugging in to the new environment.

Will this principle of "doing it badly at first" apply to crying, expressing anger, telling the story of your loss, and going through the other components of grief work? For me it has been much the same pattern, whatever the level of grief I face. I still don't always do it well, but I surely do it better. Plus, again and again I have moved to new life after feeling crushed by a disappointing loss.

Find Your New Life

When we are willing to celebrate the gift that was lost more than focusing only on the loss itself, taking another step toward renewal of life becomes possible. Sometimes successes we have had in early life can help build bridges to the new life we hope for. My father lived fifteen years after my mother's death. Even as a child I had realized that they were in love in a way I did not observe in my friends' parents. My father valued and related to my mother as an equal, doted on her, and saved sacrificially to buy her presents despite hard economic times.

At the end of her long illness, I thought for a time that my father might illustrate the axiom we see so often: when one elderly partner dies, the other will die within a year. Not so with him! After a time of numbness and loneliness, he began to reach out to other people. He told me tales of the early days of their marriage and talked profusely about my mother and what a gift she was to him. "Who do you know who had a better wife than Kathleen?" he would ask. Then he would launch another story of the grand memories he had of her when she was healthy and strong.

My father faced his grief, conceived new ways of facing life that he had never considered before, and pushed himself to move on into the unknown of his future Eight years later, when Dad was eighty-eight, he met and fell in love with Joanne, an honors English teacher in a local high school who was a year younger than I. For six years they lived and loved as if they had invented marriage. Against all the advice of those who thought the age difference was too wide to span, they had a genuinely healthy marriage—one that followed serious earlier grief for both of them.

Surprisingly, Joanne predeceased my Dad. Her metastatic breast cancer literally took her over while she was still engaged in teaching. She fought valiantly but unsuccessfully. Again I saw my father stunned and shocked. Then he began to focus on the positive celebratory memories. He would ask, "Who do you know who has had a better life than I have?" Then he would talk about Joanne and what a delight she was, his career in education, his love for the two major women in his life, and his pride in his granddaughter, her husband, and their two children.

Dad even learned to do something he did very little as I grew up. He affirmed me verbally. He spoke his love and respect for the kind of person I had become, the kind of professional I was. He gave me a blessing that candidly I never heard or felt as a teenager, though I knew in my head it was there all the while. He affirmed Ardelle and our marriage, though he had thought it a mistake at first. But, at ninety-four, the loss of Joanne was too much for him. He didn't have the strength to begin again, although he did make valiant attempts in the last few months.

An optimist all his life, my Dad marshaled the power of that optimism and Christian hope to focus on the gift rather than the loss. He thus became for me a hero all over again. He faced the grief of "deciding it was time to die," or, as he put it to a physician who wanted to install a "peg" in his stomach, "You don't seem to understand that I'm ready to get on with the next thing. You say it will prolong my life, but I think it will only lengthen my existence." My father understood that life is gift and, as Wren wrote, "It's worth is past conceiving."

Trust and Follow God

When we are willing to trust and follow God regarding our well-being and our future, we can utilize the faith and courage to take further steps into new life. Much of moving beyond grief relates to relinquishing the myth of control over one's life. Two early departures from grace related in the Bible both have to do with lack of trust in a gracious Creator God. Adam and Eve wanted to eat the forbidden fruit, which they thought would make them as wise as God (Gen 3). The builders of the tower of Babel wanted to "make a name for themselves," which they thought would provide an invulnerable defense so they would not be "scattered across the earth" (Gen 11). They all fell into sin because of refusing to trust God.

We have much less control of life than we think we do, even when things are going well and we feel the wind at our back. It's hard to relinquish this mythical sense of control when things are going well. We feel so powerful and competent. When things aren't going well, it is equally difficult to trust. We feel depleted and hopeless. We tend to think, "After what happened to me, how can I ever trust anyone again—even God?"

I invite you to consider several experiences of people I have known. Each person at one time thought the future could offer nothing but pain because of a crushing loss. Yet, each came to a reaffirmation of life and joy at the end of saying good-bye to their grief. Please remember that I know one size does not fit all. I know some people have struggled endlessly with loss and could never find release. But there are others who have found a new beginning, which illustrates and models for us all that it *is* possible to say hello to a new life after grief.

Thomas, the courageous disciple of Jesus, is a good example of this recovery of hope. So devastated by the crucifixion that he pulled into a shell of his own and withdrew completely from the other disciples, he missed the first meeting with the risen Christ (see John 20). His hurt and skepticism were high. His pain would not allow him to accept hope, even from his fellow believers who said they had seen Jesus alive. However, when he saw Jesus for himself, he fell to his knees. Furthermore he chose the highest word for God from the Old Testament and the highest word from the New Testament and put them together for the first time in an ultimate christological confession of faith about resurrection and hope for the future: "My Lord and my God!"

Trust in God can open the prisons of doubt in our minds and hearts, offer a healing balm to our hurt and discouragement, and set us free to find joy in a blessed future. It is possible.

Remember my earlier story about the businessman who was fired a few days before his retirement was to be vested? He told me later that he would never go back to the old company. He liked his new job too well!

Remember "Evelyn," a woman with grief so deep that she could not say the word "dead" about her young husband who died of cardiac arrest? Later she shared with me the joy she had discovered in her new life.

More than one minister friend has come to me having been approached by a few self-appointed dissidents from the congregation. They wanted them to leave and were willing to pay salary and benefits on behalf of the church. Again and again I have heard these ministers speak about the devastation and betrayal they felt. Repeatedly I have heard them say they could probably win a fight with this group, but they weren't up to it and didn't want to put the church they loved through such a battle. Subsequently, I have heard them say, "My new life is better than my old! I can't believe it! I love my new place. I'm a happy person again."

In one of the churches I have served, we had a saintly joyous woman who loved working with children. Now in her senior years, she continued to "sparkle" on these young lives. But her aging made it harder. One day she called and sounded discouraged. I had never heard her sound that way.

"Pastor," she began, "I'm calling to say that I must resign my work in the children's area."

"My goodness!" I exclaimed. "How could we possibly carry on without you?"

"I've just gotten too old to get down on the floor where I must be," she said. "And when I do get down it's just impossible to get back up. Please find someone to take my place as soon as possible."

I could tell she was grieving. She had lost her husband not long before. Children and church were the principal remaining joy in her life. I knew she felt that she was letting God and her church down. I visited with her several times and sought to help her unpack her grief and realize that this decision was a necessity. I kept wondering what else we could find for her to do. Before I got around to acting, she called again.

"Hardy, I have an idea! We are bound to have people who would appreciate a call from someone at the church, but you don't have time to call all those people as often as they'd like. I can't get down in the floor anymore with my children, but I can talk on the phone. Would you give me a list of people that could use a call? I'll be glad to stay in touch with them each week and let you know when they need something from one of the ministers."

From that week to the week she moved to another city to be near her son, this wonderful woman called a list of people every single week. She prayed for those people every day. She reported to the church when someone needed to be aware of a need. She lived out our concept that in our community of faith, "every member is a minister."

Shortly before her death, she told me the phone ministry had been a true joy for her—never the same delight of being with "those blessed children." She said, "I'd just rather be with children than old folks. But, you know, those old people became my friends and as we talked they helped me get ready for the step I need to take now. I am grateful that you asked me to do that ministry!" I smiled to myself that many of those "old people" were younger than she.

I smiled that she remembered it this way: that I had asked her. Actually, she had volunteered as she sought something she could do to go on with life and ministry after the loss of her husband and "her little ones." It is possible to discover a new lease on life after grief.

Finally, Houston Greenhaw, theology professor, veteran missionary in Brazil, shared an intriguing experience with me about his parents:

Since my father was wounded in WWII, his health had always been more fragile than my mother's. They had never seriously considered the possibility that she might die before he did. Then, on Sunday, May 20, 1995, as she was playing the piano for the morning service of Sunrise Baptist Church, Kerrville, Texas (a church she and Dad had helped start), she suddenly stopped playing in the middle of the second verse of "Wherever He Leads I'll Go." She took off her glasses, folded them, and placed them on top of the piano. She folded her arms and put her head down. She was unconscious by the time anyone reached her. She said nothing to anyone. She had suffered a massive brain hemorrhage. She died about two hours later without regaining consciousness.

All of this caught Houston's Dad completely by surprise. He was unprepared to live without his wife. After the period of the funeral, going through her things, and moving to an apartment, he began to feel sorry for her—for the way that she had died. He visited her grave frequently and sometimes talked to her about the pain he was feeling and about what was going on. Then, about a year and a half after her death, he wrote a letter to his son. I reprint it as it came to me in 1998 without any editing.

Dear Son,
About two months ago as I was reading the Bible and praying (my "quiet time") I was meditating (possibly "cat-napping"), whether asleep or awake, I suddenly realized that I was in Heaven. I seemed to be suspended in space. I saw no bright light, no walls nor other structures.

Everything I saw was dimly visible through a fog or smoke (a Hollywood production). As the fog grew lighter I saw a great multitude of people before me extending to the limits of view, silhouettes. I could not distinguish them except to see them as people.

They seemed to be in rows facing away from me (not as soldiers, not in straight lines).

Then the face of the nearest person (maybe 20-30 yards away) became visible. She was a young woman with such beautiful complexion, with beautiful brown hair piled upon her head (not by a hairdresser) but naturally curly.

I recognized her as Earlene. Then she turned her face toward me. Such a beautiful young woman! I knew she was Earlene. She was wearing a "meddi-blouse" patterned after the Navy's sailors in WWI. There was a large white collar and then a blouse of some kind. I did not distinguish anything else.

I smiled at her. She smiled back. Then she gave the special little wave with her hand (a wave known only to the two of us). She looked so happy. Then she looked forward again and began what seemed like a marching away of the whole group.

I called out "Whoa! Wait! Stop! That's my wife!" Then the Scriptures came to me, "There is neither marriage nor giving in marriage in heaven" (Luke 20:25, Mark 12:25). She is no longer my wife. She was so involved in activities in heaven that were so wonderful that life on earth was insignificant to her.

Then the thought came to me that the Christian's life is immortal and indestructible—"to be absent from the body is to be present with the Lord." Earlene never died! When I saw her pulse beat for the last time, she went right on into heaven. Then the thought came to me: "How could I grieve over her death when she isn't dead?"

So, from that moment on, I ceased to grieve over her but rejoiced instead. Of course, the loneliness is still there. There came to mind again the thought: she and I have together four children, eight grandchildren and any number of great grandchildren. And neither time nor eternity can take them away from us. It was

a great day and a marvelous feeling, and continues to
be a joy.

Your Dad

A year later the news came from Houston that Mr. Greenhaw
had married again. I thought to myself: he is going on with his
own life. He is very happy with his new life and new bride.[1]

We grieve in different ways. As we grieve, we are set free by
the spiritual power God gives us to accept our loss and decide to
go on with our lives. It's true that life may never be the same. Yet
it can be valid and meaningful. It can bring joy and hope.
Sometimes, as an amazing number of people have told me and as
I have experienced personally, it can even be better than the
former life.

I invite you to listen for a word from God for your grief as
you read the call, challenge, and promise of God to Isaiah. Isaiah
writes concerning the grief Israel had endured for so long as a
nation in defeat and exile. Isaiah invites those disconsolate ones
to know what the heart of God feels about their pain. He invites
them to accept the comfort of God that can lead them along the
"Holy Way" to the renewal of life. Listen for a word from God
for yourself in my paraphrase of Isaiah's words:

> The wilderness of your grief and the dry land of your
> loss shall be glad;
>> the desert of your desolation shall rejoice
>> and blossom like the crocus;
> It shall blossom abundantly,
>> and rejoice with joy and singing. . . .
> You shall see the glory of the LORD,
>> the majesty of our God.
> God will strengthen your weak hands and make
>> firm your feeble knees.
> God will say to those who are of fearful heart:
>> Be strong! Do not fear! Here is your God!
>> Your God is here!

God will come with vengeance, with terrible
      recompense
   to vanquish the enemy of grief and
      desolation.
God will come and save you from the ravages of
      your sadness!
Then the eyes that are blind to a new life will be
      opened
   and the ears that are deaf to the hope of
      good news unstopped;
Then the lame shall leap like a deer
   and the tongue of the speechless shall sing
      for joy.
   For waters shall break forth in the
      wilderness
      and streams in the desert;
   The burning sand shall become a pool
      and the thirsty ground springs of water;
   The haunt of the jackals shall become a
      swamp,
   the grass shall become reeds and rushes.
   A highway shall be there
      and it shall be called The Holy Way;
   those who have fallen in love with their grief
      shall not travel on it.
      it shall be rather for God's people who
         have let go of their grief.
   No traveler, not even fools, shall go astray
      on this road.
   No lion shall be there nor shall any ravenous
      beast come up on it
   They shall not be found there; but the
      redeemed shall walk there
      into the freedom and restoration God
         has planned for them.
   And the ransomed of the LORD shall move
      forward into new life
      and come to Zion with singing;

Everlasting joy shall be upon their heads;
they shall obtain joy and gladness,
and sorrow and sighing shall flee away.[2]

Compare this promise of God through Isaiah to the promises of God from the Psalms and the New Testament as listed in chapter 9. In reading and rereading such passages, God offers solace in our grief, and the Spirit issues a challenge for our new lives on the other side of the valley.

Notes

[1] Letter from Houston Greenhaw, 23 December 2003.

[2] Isaiah 35:1-10, paraphrased with reference to grief work.

Chapter Seven

Seeking Wholeness and Joy in Your New Life

To lose is to grieve. Grieving a crucial loss is to feel broken. People in grief often speak of "my broken heart" or "coming to pieces." We experience a feeling of being crushed internally when death, divorce, rejection, or any sort of critical loss shatters a relationship. People say, "I have lost my joy."

Some call it "falling apart." When they begin to recover, they speak of "getting it back together" or "getting back on my feet." Some speak of disintegration being replaced by integration when they heal. To heal from grief is to begin to feel whole again. To be whole again is to discover new joy. A grieving person at some point needs to know that a new life is possible.

My boyhood friend "James" lost his daughter when a drunken youth speeding in his truck at almost 100 miles an hour careened into her on a city street, crushing the small car she was driving and taking the life from her body. A short while later, James—a picture of health with no history of heart trouble in the family—suffered a massive heart attack. When I saw him in the cardiac care unit, he said, "When that boy killed my daughter, he broke my heart." Later, after the real struggle and pain, James drew upon his relationship with God and other people, recovered his equilibrium and told me "I miss her terribly, but my broken heart is well."

My friend "Thelma" was dismissed from her job without warning. She went to a meeting she thought was a routine session with her employer only to learn she was being terminated without discussion or recourse. Her first words to me were "I am devastated! She broke my heart!" Later, as her grief work took shape, she remarked in an e-mail to me, "I am beginning to feel like my old self again. I am still terribly hurt by what happened, but my broken heart is healing. I have found a new job that challenges and fulfills me. I have found a new life and new joy. My friends are telling me that they feel like the old Thelma is back."

Such healing is a matter of what some people call "regaining my equilibrium." One person said to me, "My grief knocked me off my feet, but now I feel I have my balance again." But is balance is the best word for what we seek as we recover?

My Search for an Understanding of "Balance"

For years I have pondered this: what is the best word to describe the equilibrium we seek amid grief? What do we call it and how do we get through the valley to the other side where we can regain equilibrium and discover new joy?

During my college days, Karl Menninger of the famed Menninger Clinic in Topeka, Kansas, wrote "The Vital Balance," a classic book on being a healthy person emotionally. Years later at a conference, I heard him speak about this vital balance as a way of dealing with stress. But by the 1980s—when he was well into his nineties—the great psychiatrist told us he wished he had named the book, "The Vital *Im*-Balance."[1] After all, he said, "balance" suggests both perfectionism and lack of flexibility. Balance suggests a static state of being. To have perfect balance one must be immobile at that moment. He wished for a different word to describe the dynamic state of being he had called balance in his

70

book. He wanted to avoid perfectionism and inflexibility, both of which are enemies of the equilibrium that makes for good health.

I agree! We need a better word than balance. We need help moving beyond what we lost toward both spiritual equilibrium and joy. My major guides in seeking to find equilibrium and joy at the end of grief have been the Scriptures in general and Jesus in particular. Both point to a spiritual equilibrium, which is the foundation of joy.

Jesus offers help for this quest in at least four foundational ways. Drawing from the Old Testament and his own experience with God, Jesus makes (or quotes) four statements that address where I believe we need to grow as we grieve:

- Love God with your whole self and your neighbor as yourself.
- Do this and you will live.
- I have come that you may have joy and that it may be abundant.
- Love God with your heart, mind, strength; in other words, your soul.

Love God with All You Are and Love Your Neighbor as You Do Yourself

In response to a lawyer's question about how to inherit eternal life, Jesus asks, "What do the Scriptures say?" The lawyer, quoting the Old Testament Shema, replies, "Love God with all your mind, heart, strength, soul, and love your neighbor as you love yourself."

I believe we learn three basic things about a life of equilibrium, joy, and the spiritual development of becoming a healthy self in this exchange.

(1) The basis of eternal life is to love God with your whole self. In other words, we must truly worship God as Creator and Lord—nothing less than God , nothing other than God. When God is the foundation and ultimate value of life, we may respond

to the love God gave us in creation and in Jesus Christ. When we do respond, we discover that eternal life is born of right relationship with God, self, and others more than of recovering what we lost.

(2) When we truly love God and bow before God in worship, rather than trying to use God to get what we selfishly want, we are freed to love ourselves appropriately. God helps us develop a firm, solid ego that is not selfish or egotistical. This ego is a centered self, a healthy self. Hans Selye said, "Ego*istic* is healthy; ego*tistic* is not; egotistic is destructive."[2] Or, to quote John Sanford, "Only persons with a strong ego can give up the ego; we cannot give God what we do not possess."[3]

Hence, loving self is not necessarily self-centered. Self-centered and self-centered in God are not the same thing. God loves us and wants us to love ourselves, value ourselves accurately, and take good care of ourselves. When we experience horrific loss, God wants us to recover balance and move into a new day of joy apart from that pain. As we learn to love ourselves in this sense of having a healthy ego, we can then truly love others. If I do not love myself on top of the foundation of loving God, I have no real self to give to others in love.

(3) When we love God wholly and ourselves appropriately, we are freed to love others genuinely and to value them as equals under God instead of underlings or adversaries. These three truths provide a valid basis for facing a new life after grief. But Jesus said something else to the lawyer.

Do This and You Will Live

When the lawyer answered Jesus in this way, Jesus responded, "You have spoken rightly. Do this and you will live." I believe Jesus is pointing to a broader view of "eternal life" than we generally understand.

To equate "eternal life" solely with heaven or the afterlife misses a fuller meaning of the phrase that offers both insight and healing for our grief. In other words, I do not hear the lawyer solely asking Jesus, "How may I go to heaven or how may I live forever?" as much as I hear him asking, "How may I have the kind of quality, freedom, and joy that I see in your life?" "I am a religious man," the lawyer was saying, "but my life and religion do not have the quality, nor do they furnish the joy, I see in yours."

Eternal life does speak of longevity, but first and foremost it speaks of quality, wholeness, freedom, and joy that we may experience in this present life—here and now. William Sloan Coffin Jr. says this clearly and succinctly: "We are on the road to heaven if today we walk with God. Eternal life is not a possession conferred at death; it is a present endowment. We live it now and continue it through death."[4]

When we mortals are immersed in grief, we desperately need to discover this more present meaning of "eternal life" and not see eternal life as referring only to "everlasting life." Through seeing eternal life as a godly quality of life, as well as the three basics above, God can lead us into new joy. But what does God mean by joy?

I Have Come That You May Have Abundant Joy

This present quality of eternal life offers us both freedom from the bondage of grief and genuine joy in living. It extends what George Matheson wrote in his confessional hymn "O Love That Will Not Let Me Go," which he penned after the loss of his beloved fiancée. He called it the "joy which seekest me through pain."[5]

Joy is another word that bears defining more accurately than our common usage. To the current secular mind, joy seems to mean happiness; "If I have what I want when I want it, I am happy, to be happy is to have joy." This is how our world defines joy. But joy as a spiritual quality is much deeper than this. It is not and cannot be self-oriented. Joy must be God-oriented. For me it is more than cliché to say happiness has more to do with wanting what you have than having what you want. Joy exists only in valid relationships with God, self, and others.

What did Jesus want for us when he said, "I came that you might have joy and that it might be abundant"? What does Jesus want for the grief sufferer who turns to him as comforter and guide? Let's look at the biblical concept of joy.

The Greek New Testament word for joy is *chara*. It comes from the same root as the word for grace, which is *charis*. Joy means not so much that I am happy as it means that I am in living partnership with the grace of God. In fact, there is a progression of grace built around the Greek root word *char* that helps us move from grief to joy when we choose to enter that partnership and follow the progression:

(1) Grace (*charis*) is God's unmerited favor, given freely.
(2) Gift (*charisma*) is God's special gift to every person.
(3) Joy (*chara*) is what we experience in response to receiving God's gift and putting it to a valid use in partnership with God.
(4) Thanksgiving (*eucharisto*) is how we pay the grace of God forward instead of trying to pay it back or simply to *feel* grateful.

When we move from grace to gift to joy to thanksgiving, we move into a partnership cycle with God in which we, having received God's grace and giftedness, take our joy and thanksgiving and reinvest them in the partnership process by extending grace to others.

In summary, joy is passing on to others the grace you have received from God. Joy means living your life in partnership with God as you find your niche in a vocation (not just a career or job) of being a grace giver. A job or career may be how we make a living. A vocation has more to do with how to make a life. Vocation may have little or nothing to do with earning. It has everything to do with having God as your partner and companion in living a grace-based, grace-giving, joyous life.

Summon your best imagination and look at the chart below. Try to see it not as a static group of words on a piece of paper. Allow it to become a moving circle of redemptive grace as you engage in the partnership of being a giver of grace as God is a Giver of Grace.

Start with God at the center of the page, as God is the center of your life. See God moving out of the Trinitarian triangle (as Father, Son, and Spirit) toward you with the ultimate offer of grace (*charis*). As you receive grace, you become aware that the grace is not simply forgiveness of sin, but it is the offer of special gifts as Paul mentions in 1 Corinthians 12 and Romans 12.

Visualize the dynamic, moving arrow going from grace to gift (*charisma*). Then visualize the arrow moving around the circle into joy (*chara*). Note that the way you experience this joy is not merely through accepting the grace and gifts, but through putting gifts to use in your life as a partner with God.

Be sure to use the gifts, as Jesus said, "with your mind, heart, and strength." Made in the image of God, you have a Trinitarian construct within your own giftedness. You employ these precious gifts with your intellect, your emotion, and your action as the arrow keeps moving around the circle toward grace again.

Now the arrow is moving with the momentum built from God's grace and gifts and your own joy toward thanksgiving (*eucharisto*). Note that this dynamic, moving arrow does not stop and become self-satisfied and complacent once there is an experience of joy and gratitude. The arrow keeps moving back toward the top of the page as the gratitude we feel is expressed and invested into thanks*giving*, thanks*living* with God and others.

We then take the gratitude and reinvest it in the redemptive process of being gracious to others as God was and is gracious to us. When we get personally involved in the movement of this grace-gift-joy-thanksgiving cycle, we begin to see God and life differently than when we saw these words as if they were static concepts on a page. They come alive! God comes alive in us! We come alive to ourselves and others.

God is no longer simply "someone up there somewhere" in whom I believe. God is now my leader, companion, and guide in living. Joy is not the absence of pain so much as it is the assurance of this presence and partnership with God *amid* our pain as we serve with the gifts God has given us.

Thanksgiving (*eucharisto*) is not thanks*feeling*; it is an enlistment in the joyous task of sharing grace with others as God does. We do this by giving grace to others as God has given grace to us. This is the relationship Jesus had in mind when he said, "I came that you might have joy and that it might be abundant." Abundant joy is what God wants for you following your grief.

Love God with Your Heart, Mind, and Strength

Jesus also taught us in the "Great Commandment," as we love ourselves appropriately, to take seriously three facets of our entire personality. The words *person, personality,* and *soul* are basically synonyms in the New Testament. God gave us three basic personality qualities or gifts when we were created: (1) the mind (the intellectual part of you), (2) the heart (the emotional part of you), and (3) the strength (the action part of you).

God has given us necessary equipment with which to think, feel, and act. I believe Jesus is saying that when we love God with each and every part of the personality instead of the part we use more easily, our soul meets the soul of God (see the paraphrase of Psalm 85 and the meditation in ch. 9). Our self, made in God's image, meets the self of God our Creator and Redeemer. We dis-

76

cover both wholeness and joy as we seek to utilize and integrate all three of these parts into a meaningful equilibrium.

My interpretation is that just as God's Self is Trinitarian in makeup (Father, Son, and Spirit), humans as well are trinitarian in makeup (mind, heart, and strength). These three are the component parts of my soul or my self.

Moreover, my soul, in biblical language, is not something I "have," but is someone I *am*. From the point of view of Greek philosophy, people "*have* a soul." From a biblical viewpoint my soul, made in God's image, includes my intellectual, emotional, and action strengths. This is who I am rather than something I have. My soul is my self. I *am* my soul.

Furthermore, I have found that knowing someone below the superficial level in pastoral ministry and counseling venues enables us to diagnose which component is a lead gift and which is supportive. Then we can rank these gifts according to how comfortable we are using them in our lives. We can learn which is most natural to utilize and which is most difficult, leaving the third somewhere in between.

In my case, I am confident that my mind is the easiest and most natural for me to use, my heart is next, and my strength or action strength is the last and most difficult. The order in which I use my strengths has made grief work difficult for me because I tend to overanalyze, procrastinate, fear expressing my feelings, and act too slowly. In my grief work, I have learned that I must feel and act, not just think, remember, and analyze.

When I learned to use my three basic God-given gifts in this way, I found myself having more strength and joy, and I became a more whole person. I moved beyond the fragmented person I tended to be before I consciously focused on using all three of my basic spiritual components. My relationship with God and with myself began to produce wholeness to replace the fragmentation or brokenness.

Wholeness Is What We Seek?

For me the best word for the equilibrium we need to find in our grief work—as well as in the totality of life—is the word *whole*. *Whole* is a New Testament antonym for broken; it is a psychological antonym for a fragmented, fractured self. Wholeness points to the integrity or wholeness of God on one hand and to human completeness or spiritual development on the other. Our holy God is more than different ("wholly other") from mortals. Our holy God is whole or integrated as a Self. In current jargon, God is together.

To say that God in Jesus Christ can make us whole further speaks to the gift of God to a broken human heart. Jesus repeatedly asked people, "Would you like to be made whole?" With the word *whole*, Jesus speaks of spiritual development, integration within the human self, integrity, and a wholeness of personality that makes us free, healthy, and joyous.

Jesus is the ultimate example of this kind of whole person. Having this wholeness within himself as a gift from God, Jesus constantly spoke these words of comfort and challenge to broken people: "Be made whole!"

As we strive to attain a valid blend of our basic personality components, we are spiritually freed to be the real self we were created to be. We are able to find and occupy the niche that makes us partners with God and gives us joy. Furthermore, we are empowered to become the full self God can lead us into becoming. New life can happen even for you—*if* you are willing to make the hard choice to continue growing with God into wholeness. For me, wholeness is the best word for the equilibrium we want to recover.

God wants us to be whole instead of fragmented, authentic instead of phony; God wants us to be all we can become, not just who we are now. I like the quotation a special friend cross-stitched for my office wall: "What you are is God's gift to you; what you become is your gift to God."

Sanford describes Jesus as doing precisely that: "Looked at psychologically, the Gospels reveal the personality [of Jesus as that] of a whole person. It is apparent that we have here in Jesus of Nazareth the paradigm of the whole man, the prototype of all human development, a truly individual person, and therefore someone unique."[6] Sanford also said, "Jesus took all these sides of himself seriously and gave us a model of what it means to be a spiritually healthy, whole human being."[7] To paraphrase Dorothy Sayers, the great British mystery writer and theologian, "Jesus came to reveal God as God is and human beings as God meant for us to be."[8]

Jay Thomas uses the word "blend" to describe this dynamic, creative way of being healthy. Instead of speaking of balance, Thomas agrees with Menninger and prefers to speak of "flexibility—something that is not static or immobile." Thomas asserts that "All humans are naturally out-of-balance. This is how God made us. It is natural and acceptable to be out-of-balance. It makes you who you are. And it can lead you to become who you could become when you use all your God-given strengths."[9]

When we learn that it is not the recovery of balance we seek but rather spiritual wholeness, this awareness makes the saga of a grief journey a spiritual adventure instead of an agonizing human marathon. We approach this quest for wholeness aware that our Lord was "a man of sorrows and familiar with suffering,"[10] who utilized all the strengths God gave him—heart, mind, and action. We look to Jesus as "the pioneer and perfecter of our faith."[11] Jesus has "been through weakness and testing—experienced it all," to use Peterson's paraphrase.[12] He knows what it is to struggle with loss. He knows experientially what it is to hurt, to feel lonely and out of control. Yet he continued in his own spiritual development with God, himself, and others as he "matured, growing up in body and spirit, blessed by both God and people."[13]

The Choice to Enter New Life

We walk through the valley of shadows—whatever the reason for our loss—with God the Father who created us, Jesus the Christ who died for our sins and continues to redeem us, and with the Spirit of God who is faithful to energize and accompany us in the struggle. God—as Father, Son, and Spirit—travels with us as Lord, Leader, and Companion in our journey to new life.

Much like Abraham and Sarah, we are challenged by God to go with God into "a land I will show you."[14] As fearful as this challenge can be, we can discover that whatever form this new life may take, it will be something like "the new heaven and the new earth" described in the book of Revelation. This hope is not merely a longing for the afterlife, nor for an everlasting life. It is a hope for allowing the "eternal life" of God to come alive in us here and now to make us whole and give us joy. Paul refers to this hope as an earnest type of deposit toward what we will fully receive when we are "sealed with the promise of the Holy Spirit, which is the guarantee of our inheritance until we acquire possession of it."[15]

Listen for a word from God for you in what God promised the beloved Apostle John about this hope for a new life:

> Then I saw a new heaven and a new earth,
> for the first heaven and the first earth had passed
> away.
> And there was no longer any sea
> to leave us feeling so separated . . .
> And I heard a loud voice from the throne saying,
> "Now! You will no longer be so sad and
> broken!
> The dwelling of God is now with human
> beings.
> God will dwell with us. We will be God's
> people.
> God's presence will be continually with us.

God will be our God, our Emmanuel!
God will wipe away every tear from every
     eye.
There will be no more death or mourning
     or crying or pain,
For this old order of things has passed
     away."
He who was seated upon the throne said,
     "I am now making everything new!
Write this down!
For these words are trustworthy and true!"[16]

Here I make my own confession of faith in God who is Lord of this new life that can follow the ravages of grief.

- I believe these words are trustworthy and true.
- I believe God can and will lead us into new life after grief.
- I believe we can trust God who gave us life in the first place to give us new life now—even amid a devastating loss.
- I believe this new life is a gift from God *now* just as my life in the first place was a gift.
- I believe this new life is a life of wholeness and joy.
- I believe this kind of joy and new life can begin now and will be even more fully realized as my relationship with God matures and develops beyond my death.

I wish you, my fellow seeker, good journey as you discover the wholeness and joy God wants for you when you say hello to your new life after grief.

Notes

[1] Karl Menninger, lecture at a conference on stress, Galt House Hotel, Louisville KY, 1980.

[2] Dr. Hans Selye, lecture at a conference on stress, Galt House Hotel, Louisville KY, 1980.

[3] John A. Sanford, *The Kingdom Within: A Study of the Inner Meaning of Jesus' Sayings* (Philadelphia: J. B. Lippincott Co., 1970).

[4] Ibid.

[5] William Sloan Coffin, *Credo* (Louisville: Westminster John Knox Press, 2004), 170.

[6] You may read the whole text of this hymn written by Matheson when he was in deep grief in the First Baptist Church of Greenville, SC hymnal (Macon GA: Smyth & Helwys, 2002), 277.

[7] Sanford, *The Kingdom Within*. Sanford uses the construct of the Myers-Briggs Type Indicator, which is based on the psychological types suggested by C. G. Jung, to assert that Jesus was a perfect balance of the functions discussed in this approach.

[8] Dorothy Sayers, *Creed or Chaos: Why It Really Does Matter What You Believe: A Collection of Essays on Theology*, 1947.

[9] Jay Thomas, personal letter from Dr. Thomas, 18 December 2003. Thomas takes a similar but much clearer approach than Jung or the MBTI to describe the strengths humans have as gifts from God. The Thomas Inventories of Strengths may be completed inexpensively online at their website to find out how your God-given strengths are manifested in your personality from this point of view. The Thomas website is <www.oppositestrengths.com>.

[10] Isaiah 53:3, NIV.

[11] Hebrews 12:2, RSV.

[12] Hebrews 4:15, Eugene H. Peterson, *The Message: The New Testament in Contemporary English* (Colorado Springs: NavPress, 1993).

[13] Luke 2:52, *The Message*.

[14] Genesis 12:1, RSV.

[15] Ephesians 1:14, RSV.

[16] Revelation 21:1-5; my paraphrase adapted to refer to life after grief.

Chapter Eight

Pastors Are People Who Grieve

A mong the multiple mistakes I have made as person and pastor is the assumption that I must not grieve while I help others grieve. I felt in the beginning that to be a true professional caregiver, I must postpone my grief until later.

In school, I learned that I must grieve losses some way, somehow; otherwise the grief would go underground and later erupt in unhealthy ways. However, as pastor I felt I must be strong and that showing sorrow and pain would hinder the grief of those I was assigned to help. I also feared I might be seen as a whiner or a wimp. So I lived for years with the mythology that I could help others through their grief and later face my loss and do my own grief work. What a colossal and costly mistake!

While this book is primarily for someone in grief, not for caregivers or classrooms, pastors experience particular kinds of grief. I include this chapter for two reasons. First, pastors are people who grieve. Many pastors have read the earlier edition of this book. Furthermore, people who aren't pastors need an awareness that their pastors do grieve. We need to know something of the depth of grief pastors face amid their multiple 24/7 challenges in ministry. Growing up, I wasn't aware that my pastors grieved. I thought somehow they were exempt. But I was wrong.

Although the coming Messiah was described as "a man of sorrows, acquainted with grief" (Isa 53:3), I somehow missed the need to follow the model he offered of being a wounded healer. I knew my pastors were healers. It never occurred to me that they were wounded. When Jesus came and said, "Blessed are they who mourn, for they shall be comforted" (Matt 5:4), he was saying (among other things) that in addition to being comforted by the one who "has borne our griefs and carried our sorrows" (Isa 53:4), we find solace when we make the painful choice to move outside our comfort zones and express our pain and sorrow. When we choose not to do so, we prolong and intensify our grief.

It also seems that the opposite of what Jesus said about being blessed in our grief is true: "Trapped are those who avoid grief, for they shall remain disconsolate." I found this to be true of myself in the days when I felt that a pastor is a person who must not grieve while he or she helps someone else. Therein lies a mistake that many of us—pastors or not—make. We know we must grieve, but we want to find a better time to do it.

The Genesis of a Painful Mistake

In 1961 I had been a pastor for less than a hundred days when my beloved grandmother died. Other than my parents, Nana had been my closest family member and the one I identified with the most. Our family gathered at the home place and immediately assigned me the challenge of doing the sermon at the funeral the next day. By the time I arrived, the decision seemed fixed in concrete. I had never done a funeral, but I allowed my intuitive hesitancies to be brushed aside by assurances that "Nana would be so proud of you."

I listened to the family, listened to my ego, and ignored the wisdom of my intuition. I unwisely agreed. What a mistake! I
84

thought I could delay my grief until later. Not so. Once I stepped into the pulpit, I lost complete control of my emotions and added an additional sadness to the loss of our family's matriarch. I wish I could say I learned something from this, but I did not.

Within a few weeks, three prominent leaders in our small community were lost in a private plane in a rare ice storm in the wilds of Southwest Texas. Days passed before they were found dead in the wreckage. As pastor, I was there to be the strong one. I saw my job as shepherding the others through their grief. I was close to two of the men but felt it would be inappropriate for me to show the pain I felt. I remember clearly telling myself: *Hardy! You must grieve these losses.* And then I resolved to find an appropriate time to do so later.

Thus, I established a destructive pattern for my ministry—I will be the strong one as people express their grief; later I'll grieve. For years I followed the pattern of postponing, avoiding, and repressing my feelings. For years I built up a backlog of unexpressed—and therefore unresolved—grief. While I was unaware of what I was doing to myself, the pattern took its toll on my energy and well-being. Week after week, loss after loss, funeral after funeral, I delayed my grief.

Today I know that one major flaw in this approach was the assumption that there would be time later to do the grief work I needed to do. That isn't how ministry works, even in the small church I served. The reality is that by the time I shepherded a family to a better place in dealing with their loss, another family had experienced loss. The process began all over again. This cycle continued for more than a decade.

In 1973 Ardelle and I experienced a dual loss that was harder to bear. In the same summer week, Ardelle's sister Vera Beth lost her battle with metastatic breast cancer, leaving her children—three teenagers and a young adult awaiting his wedding in two weeks. Moreover, our dear friend and mentor, Blake Smith, retired pastor of University Baptist Church in Austin, Texas, dropped dead into the arms of his son John Lee as they walked up the Law School steps at Cornell University. To add to the grief, because we were out of state attending Vera Beth's funeral, we didn't learn about Blake's death until his funeral was already over.

In early 1976, our dear friend "J. T." was diagnosed with terminal cancer. In his early sixties, he was a deacon and a stalwart, courageous leader in our community of faith. He was a member of the Texas State Legislature and a longtime prominent model of citizenship in our city. He and "Mary" were our dear friends as well as fellow church members. They were perennially young and vital. We were stunned by the news but felt sure he would win this battle.

On my birthday in May that year, Ardelle was diagnosed with a rare and multiple mesodermal sarcoma of the uterus. While the prognosis predicted a 50 percent chance of survival, we focused on the 50 percent chance of death. We were shaken to the core. Ardelle's sister had recently died of cancer. Her father's prostate cancer had spread to the bone and he was struggling mightily. We felt inundated and doomed.

In October of that year, I lost the friendship of someone who was important to me as a fellow churchman and longtime friend. We didn't yet know that Ardelle would not only survive her malignancy but thrive as she did so. We were terrified by the illness and were almost disabled by the loss of the friendship. We felt our lives were falling apart, that we had "lost control." In December "J. T." died.

As you can imagine, the pattern reasserted itself and I was strong. I promised myself I would grieve later.

The Worst Period of Grief I Ever Had

In June 1978, a litany of losses descended upon us that felt like a series of plagues from ancient Egypt.

Ardelle's father died in June. He was a superior person, father-in-law, friend, and legendary preacher. Ardelle idolized her father. He had been one of my major mentors and encouragers. His death hit us hard.

Three weeks later on July 4 weekend, Carlyle Marney, mentor, pastor and friend when I was campus minister at the University of Texas, dropped dead standing in the door of his office on his way to Furman University to speak at the Pastors School. He was only sixty years old. Again, we were out of state and didn't learn of his death until after the funeral.

On the last day of July, a young adult church member took his life. I had been close to him and his bride. We had done pre-marital counseling together before their wedding and I had met with him to discuss the pressures he felt in his new job. I was devastated. I felt I had failed him.

In September our back door neighbor and fellow Second Baptist member, a beloved senior citizen, died.

In October "Bruce," veteran deacon and loyal churchman with whom I had walked a heavy pastoral journey through his long illness, died.

In November "Sidney," a beloved friend whom we had known previously in Austin, a deacon, a load-bearing church member, died.

In December we lost Roy Bass, Ardelle's and my dear friend since college days. He and Anita were in our wedding. He was mayor of Lubbock for two terms, had been deacon chair, executive council chair, and extraordinary Bible teacher, He'd done everything that needed doing both in our local church and the denomination. Just sixty years old, Roy had a massive heart attack and never regained consciousness.

Two weeks later a beloved teacher at a local high school—a loyal churchman, a gentle, caring soul—was robbed and murdered by a young drifter to whom he offered a ride on a snowy, windy day.

In February "Roger," key man at the Lubbock Chamber of Commerce, deacon, active churchman died of a heart attack.

In April Paula, active church person, mother of my good friend and golfing buddy Paul, died after a brief illness.

In July Charlie Waters, dear friend and golfing buddy, died of cardiac arrest while at St. Simons Island in Georgia attending a National School Board Convention. In addition to being a loyal, load-bearing churchman, he had been chair of both the Lubbock and Texas State School Boards. He and Lena, in their late fifties, were close couple friends of ours.

In August Jerry Hearn, former wife of my predecessor in Lubbock, took her younger daughter to the bus station early one Thursday morning to enroll in college. It was my day off, and my son-in-law Tim and I were playing golf. We had stopped at the turn between the nine holes to get something to drink when the phone rang. I heard these dreaded words: "Yes. Would you believe he's standing right here? Dr. Clemons, this is for you." Jerry had been at lunch with a friend and mentioned a sudden, horrific headache. The friend observed "stroke symptoms" and drove her straight to the hospital. She had just been checked in to ER when they called me. Tim and I were there in ten minutes and by then she was dead. Jerry was in her early forties. I could not believe it. Another huge loss for our church and for me!

In thirteen months, our church family experienced twelve significant deaths. Not that all deaths aren't significant, but every one of these was a person with whom I had a special relationship. Several of these deaths were sudden and traumatic, including a suicide, a murder, and three cataclysmic unexpected deaths of highly visible, mid-life, dearly beloved fellow pilgrims. Our church was less than thirty years old, made up mainly of younger families whose main tie with death was through the few elderly people in the church. Dealing with so much death was deeply sad as well as terrifying.

I knew what my job was. Stay strong, weep privately, and get through this crisis before I allow myself any real grief work. Stay in control. Coach Darrell Royal had taught me that "when the going gets tough, the tough get going." I was too big a boy to cry and too nice a boy to cuss.

Waves of grief would well up within me. I would suddenly, in the middle of something important, feel an overwhelming urge to start crying. I was exhausted. I was surrounded by the families of these deceased people and eager to be there for them.

Later, I told myself. *Later I will find a time to grieve. But not now. I must be strong.*

Learning to be a Wounded Healer

You may feel overwhelmed by my long litany of loss. That is precisely how I felt as we moved from loss to loss through this nightmarish year.

Still, in the next few years I tried to make my "be strong" protocol work. I actually convinced myself that it was working. We continued to have the regular number of losses and deaths. People lost jobs, divorced, moved away, struggled with bad lab reports, were disappointed with their children or their parents, had miscarriages and still births, and were passed over for the dream job they always wanted in the public sector or the university.

Two different times in these years, two suicides occurred on the same day. On one occasion, two teenage boys who barely knew each other—totally independent of each other—took their lives within a twenty-four-hour period. One hooked up the exhaust to his car and asphyxiated himself, and the other shot himself in the head. I knew and loved each of these teenagers as well as their families. I hurt, I ached, and I was strong.

Shortly afterward, a veteran, highly respected university administrator who had served on the search committee that recommended me to the church, walked into a pawn shop across from the university and bought a hand gun, called his wife to say that he would be "a little late for lunch," and then drove to the edge of town and shot himself in the head. None of us knew he was depressed at all! We were disbelieving and horrified.

Later that night, a young husband and father who had been embarrassed at work by something stupid he had done decided he could not face his boss and coworkers. He went out in the backyard and hanged himself. I was close to each of these men as well as their families. I was stunned.

In the middle of these losses, Lena Waters, Charlie's widow and a dear friend of Ardelle's, a deacon, a highly-respected church woman, and a university professor, was diagnosed with metastatic cancer. Soon, further complications occurred. Ardelle and I sat with her three children and a team of physicians as the decision was made to remove her from life support. We stood around her bed praying, holding hands as the device was unplugged. In a few moments, she took her last breath and was at peace. We were in agony.

In 1981 my mother began a two-year debilitating decline that would end in her death the same day that "Bob," the thirty-nine-year-old mayor of Lubbock who had grown up in our church, son of "J. T. and Mary," went to the refrigerator around midnight and dropped dead of a heart attack with the glass of milk in his hand.

My perception of my assignment, as you now know, was to be strong for everyone else. You know the story by now. I am the pastor. I must be equal to the occasion—strong. I was dying inside, but I could find no adequate place or time to do my own grief. Before we got beyond one tragic loss, at least one more was there lurking.

My phone rang about 2 A.M. the next November. My friend Mark Bass, whom I have known all his life, said, "Hardy, I hate calling so late, but Grady is dead. Killed in a plane crash in Cullman, Alabama." Grady Nutt had been with our church for a four-day emphasis only two weeks before. He and I had been dear friends since he entered Wayland College, 45 miles from Lubbock, in the early 1950s. I had never lost anyone as close as Grady.

My mother died in June 1983. Blessedly, Ardelle and I had a two-week vacation scheduled in the Colorado mountains with two of our dearest friends. I thought I finally had time to unpack some of my agony. But I now know that I was still in too much shock, too numb to accomplish much with that little time. It helped, but not adequately.

Not long after that, another middle of the night call announced that Milton and Bettie Ferguson's daughter, Jo Cathy, was killed on the streets of Kansas City by a drunk driver. The Fergusons had been dear friends during and since our seminary days. Our daughter Kay and their oldest, Jane Ann, were best friends when they were little girls. We did not know Jo Cathy except as the daughter who came after we left school. But we wanted to be with Milton and Bettie, so we flew to Kansas City for the funeral.

Once we entered their home on the campus of Midwestern Baptist Seminary, I began to weep. I wept to the point I could not talk. I wept in the day and at night. I awoke at night weeping again. We were there for three days and I never stopped weeping for long. At the Ferguson home, at our dear friends' home where we stayed, on the freeways between the cities, at the service, at the graveside, and at the dinner afterward, I wept to the point of profound embarrassment. *I barely knew Jo Cathy*, I thought to myself.

Finally, the reality of what was happening occurred to me. For the first time in all these years of being with beloved people in grief, I was in a venue where I was not in charge. I was not the pastor. Nobody was looking to me. No one expected me to say some spiritual *bon mot* to address their pain. I was there without portfolio! I was "off duty." We all knew we were there to share our common grief. For the first time, I did not lay on myself the onus of being the strong one. And I lost it! I lost control. I could not stop crying.

Later, I contacted both Dr. Oates and Dr. Mahone, my counselors, friends, and supervisors. They helped me identify my grave error in assuming that I had to be the boy who kept his finger in the dike so that the dam would not break. They guided me as I began the sort of grief work I should have begun long before.

I learned in this painful saga that pastors are people who grieve. I learned that I must grieve my losses *as they occur*, that I cannot afford the luxury of postponing my pain. In that process, I am confident that I became a healthier person and a better pastor.

In ensuing years I have not postponed my grief. I have "wept with those who weep" as the Apostle Paul advised us. I have concluded, in the words of my friend Ed Bratcher, that we pastors tend to adopt for ourselves a "walk-on-water syndrome" that depletes our energy and erodes our well-being.[1] Sometimes the syndrome is encouraged by well-meaning members of our congregations. In whatever way this mantle comes, it is destructive of good pastoral and personal health. I like to remind myself that not even Jesus had a "Messiah Complex." I have learned to let grief come when it will, to deal with the embarrassment of tears and the fear of being called a weakling. I have learned better to be a wounded healer.

What I've Learned about Being a Healthier Person and Pastor

I've culled my experiences into seven lessons about the importance of grieving:

(1) *Let your personal self prevail over your professional self.* It seems more important to me to be a Christian than a pastor when I have to choose, and sometimes I have felt confronted with that choice. Paul Tournier, in four wonderful days in 1963 at Laity Lodge in Texas, told us that we must decide as pastors between being "a person or a personage."[2] Harry Emerson Fosdick, a mentor and the person about whose theology I wrote my doctoral dissertation, said it is possible and freeing to become a "Real Person."[3]

(2) *Cultivate at least two or three friendships in which you can be genuinely open and honest.* Don't "keep two sets of books" with yourself, your friends, and your church people about your emotions. I learned that they can handle my grief better than I. In fact, my grieving openly somehow gave them permission to release their own sorrows.

(3) *Practice expressing your emotions appropriately.* They will not ever come at a "good time." Emotions have an agenda of their own. You probably will have to do this unskillfully and endure embarrassment before you can do it more skillfully. But do it. No one, and certainly not God, expects you to be perfect.

(4) Get in a support group where you can be confident of the confidentiality, free to be your real self, not the leader, and in a reciprocal environment.

(5) *Once you establish sharing relationships, keep in touch and stay current with these people.* Making new old friends is exceedingly difficult. One such group I meet with still gathers every other year. We were all in Austin, Texas, in the late 1950s, but now we are scattered all over the country. Thus, we meet in the east one time and in the west the next. These are priceless relationships for me.

(6) *Cultivate the whole self you were created to be and become.* As we come to mid-life, Carl Jung says we begin to be plagued by the parts of our personalities we have neglected thus far. We tend to use the strengths and functions that come easier to us and neglect the balancing functions that would make us more whole.

(7) *Stay in a counseling, supervisory, mentoring relationship with what Wayne Oates used to call a "wise old man in your life."* Also remember, as Oates grinned and said to me in 1972, "Sometimes this wise old man is a woman, or maybe even a person younger

than you."[4] In Scott Peck's language, find a "Guide" with whom you can have a therapeutic, genuinely human relationship.[5]

As this chapter concludes, I find myself identifying with Frederick Buechner—wondering if and why anyone would care about reading my personal story. However, having presented this material on different occasions to groups of pastors, I have been encouraged from their response to take the risk. I hope my words here will have some value for those of you who share our holy, heavy assignment.

Notes

[1] See Edward Bratcher, *The Walk-on-Water Syndrome: Dealing with Professional Hazards in the Ministry* (Waco: Word Books, 1984).

[2] See Paul Tournier, *The Meaning of Persons: Reflections on a Psychiatrist's Casebook* (London: SCM Press, 1957).

[3] See Harry Emerson Fosdick, *On Being A Real Person* (New York: Harper & Brothers, 1943).

[4] See Wayne E. Oates, *The Struggle to Be Free: My Story and Your Story* (Philadelphia: The Westminster Press, 1983).

[5] See M. Scott Peck, *The Road Less Traveled: A New Psychology of Love, Traditional Values and Spiritual Growth* (New York: Simon and Schuster, 1978).

Chapter 9

Lightposts on the Journey to New Life

Introduction

I am most hesitant—unwilling, in fact—to "tamper" with Scripture. I am not a professional translator of Hebrew or Greek, and I believe we must take the Bible not literally but seriously.

Yet as a pastor and pastoral counselor, I have found that putting the Scripture in language people use on a daily basis furnishes them with fresh biblical and spiritual insights that even my limited proficiency with translating and paraphrasing Scripture can offer. As I have struggled with how to be helpful to those in my congregation, it has occurred to me that paraphrases such as the ones I have included here—read from a grieving person's viewpoint—speak profoundly healing truth.

When someone finds it difficult to turn loose of grief, God can speak through the Bible and help with the painful process of letting grief go. That must be what the Psalmist meant: "Your word, O God, is a lamp for my feet and a light to my pathway."

I invite you to look and listen for a word from God in these passages. Read them silently. Read then aloud to yourself. Read them to someone else. Read them again and again. *Listen*! Listen for a word from God.

Hebrews 12:12-29

A paraphrase with reference to grief work:

I know, my beloved child, that you have been deeply hurt.
I feel your pain, and I am confident that God feels it as well.
Lift up your tired hands, then, to the Lord!
    Let God strengthen your trembling knees!
        Keep on walking on straight paths,
      so that your limp may not lead
           to a permanent disability.
    God wants you and your grief to be fully healed!
Seek to be at peace with everyone, and seek to live a holy
           life!
Remember that Jesus said:
    How blessed are those who are pure in heart!
      They will see God!
Guard against letting your grief turn you back from the
          grace of God.
I don't want anyone to become like a bitter plant
    that grows up and causes even more troubles
        with its poison.
Be careful also that none of you falls into impurity
    or loses your reverence for God and those things God
          values.
In the strong hands of God,
    all created things will be shaken and removed,
    so that those things that cannot be shaken will remain.
Even in our trauma, let us be thankful, then.
    God has made us a part of the kingdom

that cannot be shaken.
And, thus, let us offer to God acceptable worship
    with reverence and awe!
For our God is a consuming fire who can use our pain
    to burn away dross and uncover that which is pure
        beneath it!

Ephesians 1:16-23

Paraphrased with a focus on human struggle, grief, and pain:

I have not stopped giving thanks to God for you. I have heard of your crisis; I have heard of your faith. I am remembering you constantly in my prayers, and this is what I pray:

I keep asking the God of our Lord, Jesus the Christ, the glorious Father, to give you the gift of the ever-present awareness of God's Spirit.

God's Spirit will give you the wisdom and strength you need and will also reveal God to you that you may genuinely know God personally, as well as God's immense compassion and power.

I ask that your mind may be continually enlightened to see the light of God shining into your struggle, so that you may know deep in your heart God's hope in and for you now.

I also pray that you may discover how rich are the blessings God promises you as you walk through your deep and lonely darkness.

I pray that you may know how very great is God's power constantly at work in those of us who believe.

This power working in us is the same identical power as the mighty strength that God used in raising Christ from death and seated him at God's right side.

It is the same power that moves mountains, climbs mountains, and cradles us in the Father's hand so that no possible earthly power can disrupt the touch we have with God, nor the well-being that gives us.

It is the same power that enables God to put all things under the sway of Christ and that gave Christ to the church as Lord of all things—including tragedy and loss!

This church I speak of is the body of Christ, doing Christ's work in the earth. This church is the completion of Christ's work.

It brings to completion the well-being God wants you and all the world to have. I pray God's power for you now!

1 Corinthians 15:51-58

A paraphrase with reference to grief work:

Listen, and I will tell you about a mystery.
We shall not all die! But we shall all be changed—
in a moment,
    in the twinkling of an eye,
        at the last trumpet.
For the trumpet will sound, and the dead will be raised beyond
    the reach of corruption.
And we will be utterly transformed (something like a caterpillar
    into a butterfly)!
For this perishable nature of ours must be absorbed by imper-
    ishability!
These bodies that are mortal must be embraced in immortality!
So—when the perishable puts on the imperishable, and the
    mortal puts on the immortal,
you will realize the truth of this old saying:
    Death is completely swallowed up in victory!
    O Death, where is the triumph you hoped to win?
    O Grave, where is your power to sting us?
It is sin that gives death its power.
It is the law that gives sin its strength.

All thanks be to God who gives us the victory through our Lord,
  Jesus the Christ!
For God has delivered us from
    the fear of death,
    the power of sin,
        and the condemnation of the law.

Psalm 145:13-19

A paraphrase with reference to grief:

Your ability to sustain our lives is eternal, O God!
You are in charge of our well-being forever!
The Lord is faithful to the promises he made!
    And everything God does is good!
God takes initiative to help those who are in trouble.
God uses varied sorts of divine power to lift those who have
fallen as well as those who are knocked down.
God is near to those who call;
    who call to Yahweh in sincerity.
God supplies the needs of those who honor God.
Yahweh hears our cries,
    saves us—makes us whole,
        and gives us health!

Parting Words of Jesus

Adapted from John 14
Shortly before his death, Jesus said some crucially important words to
his followers. It seems appropriate for us to hear them now:

My parting gift to you is peace, peace such as the world cannot
give. Allow God to set your troubled hearts at rest. Let God

banish your fears. I do not want you to stay in your distress. I do not want you to be daunted. You have heard me say that I am going away, but I will be coming back to you.

I have said all this while I am with you so that when I am executed, your faith will not be shaken. God is sending you another comforter—another counselor—to stand by you. He will be a friend who will help you draw upon God's strength. This spiritual friend will help you cope with life. He will nurture you, comfort you, and guide you. And he will be with you forever. He will lead you to recognize and accept what is ultimately real.

Then Jesus said:

I must be going now. I am going to show the world that I love God by doing what God has commanded me to do. Get up now. Let us leave this place.

Psalm 27:1-6, 13-14

A paraphrase with reference to grief:

The Lord is my light and my salvation; whom shall I fear?
The Lord is the stronghold of my life; of whom shall I be afraid?
When evildoers assail me, uttering slanders against me,
   my adversaries and foes, they shall stumble and fall.
Though a host encamp against me, my heart shall not fear;
   though a whole army arise against me, yet will I be confident.
One thing have I asked from the Lord, that will I seek after;
   that I may dwell in the house of the Lord all the days of
      my life,
   to behold the beauty of the Lord and to inquire in God's
      temple.
For God will hide me in a personal shelter in the day of trouble;
God will conceal me under the cover of an adequate tent; God
   will set me high and secure upon a rock.
And now my head shall be lifted up above my enemies round
   about me;

and I will offer in God's sanctuary sacrifices with shouts of joy.
I will sing and make melody to the Lord . . . .
I believe that I shall see the goodness of the Lord in the land of
the living!

Wait for the Lord; be strong, and let your heart take courage;
Yea, wait for the Lord!

Revelation 7:13-17, 11-12

A paraphrase relating to grief and tribulation:

As we stood around that great white throne of God, one of the elders said to me, "Who are these people who are arrayed in white robes? From whence do they come?"

And I said to him, "Lord, only thou knowest."

God said, "Yes! I know them. These are my children who have come out of great tribulation. Now they have washed their robes, and they have become clean in the blood of the Lamb."

Therefore, they are now before the throne of God. They serve God continuously in God's temple. God who sits upon the throne shall dwell with them.

Because of God they shall hunger no more, neither shall they thirst; the sun will burn them no longer, nor will any heat they have formerly experienced.

For the Lamb that is in the midst of the throne will keep on feeding them. He shall care for their every need. He shall lead them unto the fountains of refreshing waters; and God personally shall wipe away every tear from their eyes.

All the people stood around the throne and kept on worshiping God. They kept saying: "Amen! Blessing! and Glory! and Wisdom! and Honor! and Power! and Might! be unto our God forever and ever!"

Psalm 85

Paraphrased for someone in grief:

I ask you, O God, to make me well and strong again, and I, your chosen child, in whom you have great delight, will then be able to praise and serve you.

I can't let go of my grief without trusting in your constant love, O God. I've got to have your saving help.

I'm now willing to listen to what you're saying to me. I'm willing to act with my own response.

You have promised me genuine peace if I do not keep going back to my foolish, destructive ways.

But my grief seems more comfortable and less scary than the healthy new ways you offer me. Letting go of my grief seems so frightening and painful.

I can count on the fact that you, O God, whose personal name is Yahweh, are ready to give me genuine joy and well-being.

Yet, I know that even you, O God, cannot do this if I will not cooperate by trusting God alone for my health and new life as well as making the choice to go on living. Yahweh will give me the gift of well-being, or, in other words, God's saving presence.

Yahweh promises me: my own Self will be here for you; I will be absolutely trustworthy.

Yahweh has assured me: "I will remain with you in the world. I will remain in a seeking, caring, comforting, challenging posture toward you, my child."

But I also know that even God's gift is absolutely useless and has no ability to make me well and strong, apart from my own willingness to respond with action to a personal relationship with God who gives this gift. When I do respond in my thoughts, feelings, and actions—in my mind, heart, and strength—with repentance and faith, then God's love and my faithfulness truly *meet and embrace.*

Meditation on Psalm 85

Psalm 85 is a dramatically significant passage of Scripture. As I have faced losses that left me in devastation and terror, I have turned to its pages and heard a word from God that sounds like this:

When I have lost something or someone and am inundated by the ravages of grief, I have discovered that I must respond in repentance to the God who created me, redeemed me, and accompanies me in my grief. Repentance in the language I grew up with means remorse, feeling guilty, being sorry about something. In biblical language, however, repentance is not a feeling type of word; it means to *turn*. It is a navigational term that means to turn toward God, to turn away from myself and from my loss. I have discovered that in an appropriate time of grief work, such a turn becomes possible.

I have learned that when I respond with this "turning kind of repentance," I can turn away from my loss, turn away from my love of my grief, from my fear of the future, and actually turn toward God in trust. Turning toward God is like turning toward the hug the prodigal son received when he returned from the far country into the waiting arms of the father. When I turn toward God, I turn toward the gift of new life and new joy as the son returning home did. I am then included in a new partnership after a devastating experience.

Such turning is done by grace through faith. The courage of faith that trusts God alone for my well-being enables God to do for me what I would not allow God to do before faith and repentance were exercised. I receive God's grace through exercising my faith. Such faith is a verb, not a noun. Such faith speaks of relationship and trust more than belief and understanding.

The psalmist says that when such faith is acted out in repentance, "God's love and my faithfulness truly meet, righteousness and peace will embrace" (Ps 85:10). When such a rendezvous happens with God, who shares my deepest grief, resurrection and renewal can then happen.

My human loyalty will reach up in the response of trust from the earth; God's ability to make me whole, new, and at peace gently descends upon me and into me as a gift from above. Yahweh gives me true well-being as a gift. I welcome the wholeness God offers, and the gift is consummated.

Yahweh causes my personality and my vocation of being God's partner to prosper with the richness of a bounteous harvest. My newfound relationship with Yahweh provides a path for God to enter my personality on a continuing basis. Yahweh and I become—in an even deeper way than before my loss—companions, friends, and partners in living. God is not just someone I believe in. God becomes someone whom I know and trust, someone with whom I share the journey of life.

Furthermore, my newfound strength enables me to relate to others, so that we may share our common griefs. Whatever my "job" is, however I earn my paycheck, I keep learning that the major meaning of my life is to be on vocation with Yahweh. My joy in life takes the shape of sharing the grace with others that God has given me. Receiving God's grace enables me to be gracious to others.

At the deepest level, to say good-bye to grief is to say hello to God. To say good-bye to grief is to experience a new and deeper relationship with God, who becomes your personal friend as well as your lord and leader.

To know that God loves me and will not allow anything—anything at all—to separate me from God is to know that God is the only truly constant reality in life (see Rom 8:37-39). Faith, hope, and love abide! The greatest of these is love! (1 Cor 13:13)

Conclusion

After reading these paraphrases, I suggest that you read them in your favorite translation of the Bible. Read them in Today's English Version, usually called the Good News translation. Read them in the New Revised Standard Version. Read the New Testament passages in Eugene Peterson's recent paraphrase, *The Message*. Read and reread these passages and listen for a word from God to speak to you, your grief, and your need.

These passages offer real hope and genuine help for someone who is at the point of being ready to say good-bye to grief of long standing and hello to a new life. I recognize that this is a difficult area to discuss helpfully because people in the grief process are in so many different places in their journeys. We occupy many different levels of readiness either to grieve or to let go of grief when the time comes.

What I am saying is designed to be helpful to someone who is at the point of staying too long with grief and at the point of being ready to move past grief into the reestablishment of life. I am aware that some of you may not be at that point. I have learned this with my personal grief as well as with that of people whom I have sought to help as a pastor and grief counselor. One cannot rush or take short-cuts to the point at which it becomes possible, appropriate, and necessary to say good-bye to grief and hello to life after grief.

Take your time, but do not think time will cure grief in and of itself. Embrace your pain rather than avoid it. Express your feelings rather than hide them. Let me invite you to move outside your comfort zone as Abraham and Sarah did when they launched out into a land with which they were not familiar. Remember the words of Jesus: "You're blessed when you feel you've lost what is most dear to you. Only then can you be embraced by the One most dear to you."[1]

Note

[1] Matthew 5:4, Eugene Peterson, *The Message* (Colorado Springs: NavPress, 1993), 15-16.

Appendix

Helps in Doing Grief Work

It is normal to:
  (1) feel like crying and to cry.
  (2) be angry and feel hostility—in general, at God, or even at the deceased.
  (3) feel guilty and/or regretful.
  (4) want to give up.
  (5) be dependent.
  (6) be weak and need help.
  (7) continue grieving after a long time.
  (8) say good-bye at some point—to your loss and to your grief about your loss.
  (9) reestablish and go on with your life.
  (10) return to happiness as your basic way of being.

It is not generally healthy to:
  (1) try to be or seem to be too strong.
  (2) try to avoid reality—with isolation, activity, drugs, alcohol, eating, etc.
  (3) try to shield or protect each other from pain.
  (4) drop out of your community of faith.
  (5) see God as being aloof from your pain and struggle.
  (6) try to change too much about your life too quickly.

(7) try to get over your grief too quickly.

(8) return to normal activity too soon.

(9) postpone emotions that come unbidden.

(10) isolate children from the family experience of loss and grief.

(11) continue grief indefinitely.

In times of grief, try not to say:

(1) "This is the will of God."

(2) "This is punishment for your sins."

(3) "God took your mother because . . ."

(4) "God needed another little flower in his garden, so he took your child."

(5) "There must be a reason we don't understand."

(6) "Time will heal your wounds."

(7) "Just stay busy, that's all you need."

(8) "Don't cry." "Don't let the children see you cry." "We've got to be strong."

(9) "Now you're the man of the house." "Now you've got to be the mommy here."

(10) "You mustn't feel that way." "Don't be mad at God." "It doesn't make sense to be mad at _____." "You shouldn't feel guilty."

(11) "Here, take this sedative. You'll feel better."

(12) "I once knew a person who had exactly the same thing happen." "One time I had the same experience."

(13) "I know exactly what you are feeling."

(14) "You'll get to feeling better soon."

(15) "Just pray about it and read your Bible. It'll get better."

(16) "We'll get you another dog." "You'll find another job." "You'll meet someone else." "You're young enough to have another child."

Jehovah Speaks of Life

by Hardy Clemons

Poets speak of trees that fall,
    Broad and straight and high—
Leaving gaps of emptiness,
    Leaving slots of loneliness,
        Leaving a mute evidence
That we all must die.

Poets speak of muffled oars
    Stealing through the deep—
Seeking heaven, a higher home,
    Seeking rest and joy and peace,
        Saying quietly in the gloom
That death is but sleep.

God speaks not as do the poets
    Jehovah speaks of life!
Life that lives beyond the grave,
    Life in God that will not die,
        Life victorious, transformed,
Eternally endowed!

For Adam's breath is born of God.
    God made us; and God makes
Life to spring within our breasts,
    Life to flame as in response,
    Life that lives, though all else dies,
Triumphant in God's power!

The life of our beloved one
    Is not a fallen tree.
Born of God; thrice born is she.
    She is not dead.

She does not sleep.
  She has not gone away.
She lives! Eternally in God!
  She rises powerful o'er the tomb!
  She shares God's life today!

There She Goes/Here She Comes

by Henry Van Dyke

I am standing on the seashore.

A ship at my side spreads her white sails to the morning breeze and starts for the blue ocean. She is an object of beauty and strength, and I stand and watch until at last she hangs like a speck of white cloud just where the sea and sky come down to mingle with each other.

Then someone at my side says, "There she goes!"

"Gone where?" Gone from my sight . . . that is all.

She is just as large in mast and hull and spar as she was when she left my side and just as able to bear her load of living freight to the place of destination.

Her diminished size is in me, not in her.

And just at that moment when someone at my side says, "There she goes!" there are other eyes watching her coming and other voices ready to take up the glad shout, "Here she comes!"